THE ANALYSIS OF FACTORS INFLUENCING LEVERAGE OF TANZANIAN COMPANIES

Lucky Yona

authorHOUSE®

AuthorHouse™ UK
1663 Liberty Drive
Bloomington, IN 47403 USA
www.authorhouse.co.uk
Phone: 0800.197.4150

© 2018 Lucky Yona. All rights reserved.

No part of this book may be reproduced, stored in a retrieval system, or transmitted by any means without the written permission of the author.

Published by AuthorHouse 07/23/2018

ISBN: 978-1-5462-9559-4 (sc)
ISBN: 978-1-5462-9558-7 (e)

Print information available on the last page.

Any people depicted in stock imagery provided by Getty Images are models, and such images are being used for illustrative purposes only.
Certain stock imagery © Getty Images.

This book is printed on acid-free paper.

Because of the dynamic nature of the Internet, any web addresses or links contained in this book may have changed since publication and may no longer be valid. The views expressed in this work are solely those of the author and do not necessarily reflect the views of the publisher, and the publisher hereby disclaims any responsibility for them.

The Analysis of Factors Influencing Leverage of Tanzanian Companies

Dissertation

To obtain the degree of
Doctor of Philosophy
At the E.H.E. European University EurAka, Switzerland
Under Authority of Pro-Vice Chancellor -Prof Dr Klaus Oestreicher
To be defended in Public on 27 June 2018

By Lucky Yona
DBA/MBA/MPhil/CPA/BCOM/BTH
Born in Tanzania

This dissertation is approved by the Doctoral Supervisors:

Supervisors;
Prof. Dr Jonathan Njoku – Statmind Institute, Nerthelands
Prof Robert Goedegeebure - Statmind Instistute, Nerthelands

Readers:

Prof Dr Joop Remme, Netherlands Centre of Governance
Prof Dr Dileep Kumar, Berjaya University, Malaysia

Composition of the Evaluation Committee
Prof Dr Klaus Oestreicher– E.H.E. European University EurAka Switzerland.
Prof. Dr Joop Remme, Netherlands Centre of Governance
Prof. Dr Dileep Kumar, Berjaya University, Malaysia

DECLARATION STATEMENT

I hereby declare that this research paper is my original work, which has not been submitted either in the same or a different form to this or in any other university degree.

Lucky Yona

Tanzania
June 2018

Contents

DECLARATION STATEMENT vii
ACKNOWLEDGMENT xix
ABSTRACT xxi

CHAPTER ONE 1
BACKGROUND 1
   1.1 Introduction 1
   1.2. Overview of Tanzanian Economy (2007-2014) 2
   1.3 Tanzania Capital Market and Financial Market Development 3
   1.4. Characteristics of Tanzanian Companies 5
   1.5. Statement of the Research Problem 6
   1.6. Research Objectives 8
   1.7. Research Questions 8
   1.8. Significance of the study 9
   1.9. Scope and limitation of the Study 10
   1.10. Organization of the Report 10

CHAPTER TWO 12
LITERATURE REVIEW 12
   2.1. Introduction 12
   2.2. Capital Structure definition, relevance and measurement 12
   2.2.1 Modigliani Miller Arguments 14
   2.3.2. Static Tradeoff Theory 16
   2.3.3. Pecking Order Theory 18
   2.3.4. Organizational life stage theory 20
   2.4. Capital Structure Theories link with Company Leverage 21
   2.5. Summary of Theories, Assumptions, conclusion, and Relevance 24
   2.6. Empirical Literature 25

  2.6.1. Justification on Selection of Capital structure determinants 25
  2.6.2. Determinants of capital structure 26
 2.7. Research Gap 34
 2.8. Key Issue, lessons learned and Conclusions 35

CHAPTER THREE 36
RESEARCH METHODOLOGY 36
 3.1. Introduction 36
 3.2 Research Design 36
 3.3. Conceptual Framework 37
 3.3.1 Operationalization of research variables 38
 3.3.2. Independent Variables 38
 3.3.3 Dependent Variables 47
 3.4. Research Hypotheses 48
 3.5. Hypothesis Testing 52
 3.6. Research Coherence 53
 3.7. Model Development 54
 3.8. Study Area 56
 3.9. Study Population 57
 3.10. Sample Size and Sampling Technique 57
 3.11. Data Collection Method 58
 3.12. Data Analysis 58
 3.13. Multicorreleranity Tests 60
 3.14 Ethical Consideration 60
 3.15 Summary and Conclusion. 60

CHAPTER FOUR 61
RESEARCH FINDINGS 61
 4.1 Introduction 61
 4.2. Summary Statistics 61
 4.3. Findings: Degree of Leverage of Unlisted and Listed
  Companies in Tanzania 62
 4.3.1 Introduction 62
 4.3.2 Summary Statistics 63
 4.3.3 Hypothesis Testing 70
 4.3.4 Discussions on Research Findings 71
 4.3.5. Conclusions 72

*4.4. Research Findings: The influence of Liquidity on
Company Leverage* 73
4.4.1 Summary statistics 73
4.4.2. Hypothesis testing 76
4.4.3 Discussions on Research Findings 80
4.4.4. Conclusions 81
*4.5 Research Findings: The Influence of Profitability and
Company Leverage* 82
4.5.1 Summary Statistics 82
4.5.2 Hypothesis testing 88
4.5.3 Discussion on Research Findings 93
4.5.4 Conclusions 94
*4.6 Research Findings: The Influence of Tangibility and
Company Leverage* 95
4.6.1. Summary Statistics 95
4.6.2. Hypothesis testing 99
4.6.3 Discussion on Research Findings 103
4.6.4 Conclusions 104
*4.7. Research Findings: The Influence of Company Size and
Company Leverage* 105
4.7.1. Summary Statistics 105
4.7.2 Hypothesis testing 109
4.7.3. Discussion to the Research Findings 114
4.7.4. Conclusions 114

CHAPTER FIVE 116
SUMMARY, CONCLUSIONS AND RECOMMENDATIONS 116
5.1 Introduction 116
5.2 Summary of the thesis 116
5.3 Significance of the study 120
5.4 Limitation of the Study 121
5.5. Conclusions and Recommendations 121
5.6. Further Research direction 124

REFERENCES 127
APPENDICES 139

List of Tables

Table 1.1 Selected Economic Indicators (Years: 2007-2014) 3
Table 2.1 Predicted Sign of Relationship between Variables and Capital structure Theories... 21
Table 3.1 Proxy Measurement of Independent Variables 47
Table 3.2. Proxy Measurement for Dependent Variable 48
Table 3.3. Hypothesis Techniques 53
Table 3.4 Research Coherence 53
Table 3.5- Sampling Frame- Selected Companies 57
Table 4.1 Summary Company Financial position (Assets) in Million Tshs 64
Table 4.2: Summary of Company Financial Positions (Equity + Liabilities) 65
Table 4:3. Trend Analysis: Debt to Equity Ratio 67
Table 4:4: Trend Analysis: Debt- Ratio... 68
Table 4.5: Degree of Leverage of Listed and Unlisted Companies........ 70
Table 4.6: T-tests between Listed and Unlisted Companies Capital Structure 71
Table 4.7: Descriptive statistics of Liquidity Ratios..............................74
Table 4.8 Trend analysis of Current Ratios (2007-2014) 74
Table 4.9: Regression Model with Variance Inflation Factor................ 76
Table 4.10: Correlation between current ratio and Leverage 77
Table 4: 11- Variation of the Regression Model – Debt to Equity 77
Table 4.12. ANOVA: Company Liquidity and Debt to Equity Ratio..... 78
Table 4.13 Regression- Liquidity and Debt to Equity Ratio Multicolliearnity tests -Coefficients 78
Table 4.14 - Variation of the Regression Model – Debt ratio 79
Table 4.15. ANOVA: Company Liquidity and Debt Ratio 79

Table 4.16: -Regression- Liquidity and Debt Ratio Multicolliearnity tests -Coefficients 80
Table 4.17: Descriptive statistics of Return on Equity (ROE) 83
Table 4.18: Descriptive statistics of Return on Assets (ROA) 83
Table 4.19: Trend Analysis of Return on Equity (ROE) 84
Table 4.20: Trend Analysis of Return on Equity (ROE) 87
Table 4.21: Regression Model with Variance Inflation Factor 88
Table 4.22: Correlation Analysis between Profitability ratios and Leverage Ratios 89
Table 4: 23 - Variation of the Regression Model – Debt to Equity 90
Table 4.24. ANOVA: Company Profitability and Debt to Equity Ratio 90
Table 4.25 Regression- Profitability and Debt to Equity Ratio Multicolliearnity tests -Coefficients 91
Table 4: 26 - Variation of the Regression Model – Debt to Equity 92
Table 4.27: ANOVA: Company Profitability and Debt Ratio 92
Table 4.28 Regression- Profitability and Debt Ratio Multicolliearnity tests -Coefficients 93
Table 4:29 Descriptive statistics of Companies Tangibility 96
Table 4.30: Trend Analysis of Asset Tangibility 97
Table 4.31; Regression Model with Variance Inflation Factor 99
Table 4.32: Correlation Analysis – Fixed assets Tangibility and Leverage 100
Table 4:33 - Variation of the Regression Model – Debt to Equity 100
Table 4.34. ANOVA: Company Tangibility and Debt to Equity Ratio 101
Table 4.35 Regression- Tangibility and Debt to Equity Ratio Multicolliearnity tests -Coefficients 101
Table 4:36 Variation of the Regression Model – Tangibility and Debt Ratio 102
Table 4.37. ANOVA: Company Tangibility and Debt Ratio 102
Table 4.38. Regression- Tangibility and Debt to Equity Ratio Multicolliearnity tests -Coefficients 103
Table 4.39: Descriptive statistics of Companies Tangibility 106
Table 4.40: Descriptive statistics of Sector Size (Log of Sales) 106
Table 4:41 Trend Analysis of Companies Net sales 108

Table 4.42: Correlation Analysis – Company size and Leverage 110
Table 4:43 - Variation of the Regression Model – Company Size and Debt to Equity Ratio 111
Table 4.44. ANOVA: Company Size and Debt to Equity Ratio 111
Table 4.45 Regression- Company Size and Debt to Equity Ratio Multicolliearnity tests -Coefficients 112
Table 4:46 Variation of the Regression Model – Company Size and Debt Ratio 112
Table 4:47 ANOVA: Company size and Debt Ratio 113
Table 4.48. Regression- Company Size and Debt Ratio Multicolliearnity tests -Coefficients 113

List of Figures

Figure 3.1. Study Conceptual Framework 37
Figure 4.1 Debt to Equity Ratio of Tanzanian Companies.................. 67
Figure 4.2 Debt Ratio of Tanzania Companies 68
Figure 4.3. Tanzanian Companies Current Ratios (Year 2007-2014)... 75
Figure 4.4: Return on Equity for Listed and Unlisted
  Companies (2007-2014). 85
Figure 4.5: Return on Assets for Listed and Unlisted Companies
  (2007-2014)... 87
Figure 4.6: Company Tangibility Ratio (2007-2014). 98
Figure 4.7: Trend Analysis of Company Size (2007-2014) 109

ACKNOWLEDGMENT

The whole process of accomplishing my thesis writing has not been easy but very challenging and involving. I thank God the creator and the provider of grace who gave me the ability to accomplish this work.

The support of different people is also very appreciated as it has enabled me to finish this demanding process. My greatest gratitude is deserved for Prof Jonathan Njoku, Prof Goedegeebure of Start Mind (Nerthelands) for their supervision and professional guidance. I would like to thank the two readers of the thesis: Prof Dr Joop Remme of Netherlands Centre of Governance and Prof Dr Dileep Kumar of Berjaya University, Malaysia. Sincere appreciation also goes to Professor Ven Mvano of ESAMI, for their professional challenges while writing this thesis.

My sincere appreciation goes to my entire family which includes wife Gloria and children who gave me moral support during the period of working on this dissertation. I would like also to appreciate all members of Arusha Christian Worship Centre for their prayers and support. May God bless every person mentioned here and those not mentioned who made this thesis as a success.

Lastly, I would like to appreciate Professor Bonard L. Mwape, Director General of ESAMI for giving me time to undertake my studies.

ABSTRACT

The dominant capital structure studies across the globe have been concentrated in developed countries and specifically for listed companies and few on unlisted companies or mixed companies. This thesis aims to examine the extent to which company liquidity, profitability, tangibility and company size influences the leverage of Tanzanian companies as suggested by Pecking Order and Trade off theory.

More specifically, this study adopts quantitative methods to analyze the extent to which liquidity, profitability, tangibility and company Size influences the leverage of Tanzanian companies. Panel data were collected from both listed and unlisted companies in Tanzania for period of seven years beginning 2007 to 2014.

The study findings show a negative relationship between company liquidity and company leverage as measured by debt ratio and debt to equity ratio. These findings show the validity of the pecking order theory in Tanzania. The postulates of the trade-off theory as far as liquidity is concerned are not valid. The study findings also reveal a positive relationship between profitability and leverage suggesting that majority of Tanzanian companies used more debts as the means of financing their business operations despite of their profitability. These findings are backed up with the existence of few companies that are listed in the stock exchange that are able to raise funds through equity funds.

The study found that the Tangibility of listed companies was higher than that of the unlisted companies and there was a negative relationship between Tangibility and leverage which is valid to Pecking order but contrary to trade off theory. This suggests that the majority of Tanzanian companies had adequate fixed assets for collateralization and hence allowed these companies to use debts as the means of financing their business operations. As far as company size is concerned study findings suggest that Pecking order theory (POT) and Trade off Theory (TOT) relevance cannot fully supported in Tanzanian companies as the findings have revealed a negative relationship between company size and leverage.

Based on the findings on liquidity the study used only one variable to measure liquidity (Current ratio against two variables of dependent variable (debt ratio and debt equity ratio). Therefore, conducting a further research based on use of more variables indicators of liquidity and leverage could result into different findings and conclusions. Since the study did not not establish the reasons for the decline in return on assets and return on equity for Tanzanian companies. Further research on what really influences profitability of Tanzania companies over time is needed in order to establish the causes of such major declines and develop strategies to enhance the company profitability. Further research study is needed to investigate what kind of Policies or strategies are needed in Tanzania to encourage more companies to access funding through equity.

The study did not establish the relationship between short term assets tangibility and leverage of Tanzanian companies. This suggest that further studies could be necessary to understand the relationship between short term assets tangibility and leverage. The study did not confirm on the relationship of tangibility with other capital structure theories hence a suggestion for further study.

As far as the relationship between company Size and Leverage the study used only one measures of company size namely log of Sales in this particular study. The use of different indictors of company size is likely to give different results hence a need for further research which might give different conclusions which may concur to the predictions of the pecking order and trade off theories.

CHAPTER ONE

BACKGROUND

1.1 Introduction

Capital structure studies have been carried over in many countries around the world over a period. Modigliani and Miller (1958) developed the irrelevancy theory which emphasized on financing the business activities with any source without fearing that the value of the firm could be affected. In other words, they assumed that the value of the firm remains unaffected by any financing choice method selected by Managers. The irrelevancy theories did not believe in the imperfection of markets but thought on the existence of a perfect market where there are no corporate and personal taxes) debt financing or equity financing does not influence the value of the firm. Irrelevancy theories further assumed that in the perfect market there is a free flow of information and no information costs. There is also divisibility of shares, no transaction costs such as flotation costs and there is rationality of decisions by participants as they try to maximize their profits and minimize their losses. They also further (Modigliani and Miller 1963) proved that such capital structure decisions affect the value of the company. With time, scholars came up with new theories such as the agency theory (Jensen & Meckling, 1976), Pecking Order (Ross, 1977) and the trade-off (Myers & Majluf, 1984) which relaxed assumptions of Modigliani theories as they stated new issues that affect capital structure of companies. These theories have shed more lights on capital structures of companies across the globe especially in the developed world. Capital structure studies across countries started on large listed manufacturing industries and later extended to other sectors.

Further developments on this subject are studies on determinants of capital determinants across the globe, trying to explain what influences capital leverages of various companies. The reviews are global though there are few studies on the subject of capital structure in African countries such as those by Stephen, 2010; Olayinka 2011 Olajapo, 2011; and Odit, 2011. At the same time existing literature show that the studies paid more attention to listed companies. Typical examples of studies of capital structure worldwide that seem to put less focus to unlisted companies and put much emphasis on listed companies include research on listed companies in Singapore (Lim et al., 2009), (Seealanatha, 2010), GCC countries (Wafaa, 2010) and Pakistan (Khan 2010). Another study on capital structure studied for developing countries is a study by Booth et al. (2001) who used a sample of only listed companies from ten developing countries which included Zimbabwe, India, Brazil, Pakistan South Korea, Malaysia, Jordan, Mexico, Thailand, and Turkey.

This study on the influence of capital structure determinants in Tanzania cannot be the only study; few studies already undertaken in Tanzania on the capital structure have used a sample of few companies to provide their conclusion results. A survey for example by Bundala and Machogu (2012) used a sample of only eight companies. The use of a small number of businesses in the previous study provides room for academic criticisms as to the basis of the findings and conclusions hence a need to pursue further research by using a larger sample of both listed and unlisted companies that are likely to produce different result findings. This study used a large number of data from both unlisted and listed companies as compared to previous studies which used a small sample but again only from listed companies.

1.2. Overview of Tanzanian Economy (2007-2014)

The economic indicators surrounding a country are the key factors that are likely to influence the way in which a company can raise its funds to finance its business activities. During the period of study, Tanzanian economy is explained by the variation in some of the key indicators which might have also influenced the performance and funding characteristic of business in the country. The economic indicators show a small increase in GDP growth rate from 6.2% in 2007 to 7.9% in 2011 and then a decrease to 6.8% in 2014. Such growth rate is also revealed in the GDP per capital which changed from $ 538 (2007) to $ 1044(2014) indicating that Tanzanian per capital income increased in that period. This could be a sign of increased economic activities among individuals and corporate entities. The inflation rate has not remained constant over the years but kept changing throughout the period ranging from 6.2% (2007), 5.9% (2008), 5.9% (2009). From 2010 the inflation rate increased from 6.2% to 7.8% in 2013 and dropped to 6.1% in 2014. Inflation rates influence the interest rates as well and cost of doing business which also might affect the funding of business operations. Interest rates which have a more significant influence on lending and borrowing indicated positive and negative changes at different times in the same period of study. Tanzania population has not remained stagnant over time. The population grew from 39.2 million in 2007, 40.2 million in 2008, 43.64 million in 2009, 44.97 million and 48.20 by the end of the year 2014

Table 1.1 Selected Economic Indicators (Years: 2007-2014)

Variable	2007	2008	2009	2010	2011	2012	2013	2014
GDP Growth rate (%)	6.2	6.4	6.4	6.5	7.9	6.9	7.0	6.8
GDP Per Capita ($)	538.4	663	674.8	707.9	771	818	896	1044
Inflation (End of Year)	6.2	5.9	5.9	6.2	6.8	9.6	7.8	6.1
Population Growth	39.2	40.2	43.64	44.97	45.35	46.55	47.40	48.20
Interest Rates	16.07	14.98	15.03	14.35	14.96	15.46	13.60	16.2

Source: Author Compilation from Bank of Tanzania Reports

1.3 Tanzania Capital Market and Financial Market Development

According to Komba (1999), majority of businesses in Tanzania in all sectors has gone through a long history of different phases and challenges which had a tremendous impact on their capital structure financing. During the period between the 1970s as the results of economic underperformance, companies (Komba, 1999) challenges included the lack of foreign exchange, inadequate working capital, poor infrastructure, lack of technology, weak and unsupportive financial and legal framework. During the same period, the primary source of funding for these companies was debt and own equity not raised through stock exchange mechanism as no stock market existed at that time. The nature of Tanzanian companies as explained above has its challenges when it comes to the collection of data for analysis.

Capital structure studies in Tanzania are few, but a number of those available have investigated how firm characteristics influence the firm performances such as profitability and other performance indicators. The purpose of our study is not to come up with a new theory but to contribute to the literature on the capital structure by revealing the level of gearing of unlisted and listed companies in Tanzania and explains whether different capital structure determinants influence company leverage of Tanzanian companies. At the same time, few studies on the subject matters from developing countries such as Tanzania do not give profound insights to scholars, academicians and practitioners to understand and know whether capital structure determinants influence leverage measures.

This study will use data from Tanzanian companies for a longer duration of seven years (2007 -2014) which justifies the change of financing patterns of Tanzanian companies. In this period the capital and financial market had deepened enough to allow companies to raise funds by using different sources of funds such as stock listing and securing long-term debts from commercial banks. Within this period, for example, the business banks in Tanzania increased in terms of numbers and they came up with different financial products allowing companies to have access to loans funding.

Detailed analysis of the previous studies as revealed in the literature also show that debt to equity ratio and debt ratio was used as the measure of company leverage. However, these studies majored in developing countries and few studies in less developed countries. There are inadequate studies in Tanzania that have applied the same measures of leverage. In the end, this study will add value to the body of knowledge and literature on capital structure determinants in more countries other than from only developed countries where capital structure determinants were initially tested. The study will add to the literature gap and will shed light on scholars and academicians on the subject matter. This study is also essential, as it will entail the testing of applicability of the Trade-off and pecking order theories on capital structure determinants in a less developed country like Tanzania as most of the previous studies have originated and tested in developed countries where the economic environment is different.

1.4. Characteristics of Tanzanian Companies

Tanzania has different companies that operate in different economic sectors and industries. These companies are large, and some are small. Among these companies, there are those which are listed on the stock exchange, and they are capable of raising their funds through stock listing and debts while those companies which are not listed they can only grow funds by using their internal sources (Retained earnings) as well as raise funds by taking debts from financial institutions. Tanzanian companies have different challenges of raising funds through equity or debt funding. The small companies cannot quickly issue shares to the public as listing conditions are difficulty to meet such as having minimum capital of five hundred Million Tanzanian Shillings (Equivalency of $300,000) and having profitability history of three years before listing and many other conditions. Same small companies are likely not to obtain loans from commercial banks because of high banks borrowing interest rates. The large companies in Tanzania do not have the challenges of raising funds through debts or equity funding. Despite the fact that these companies are capable of growing funds through the stock listing majority of these companies have not been listed on the stock exchange. Majority of the large companies are privately owned and because the shareholders of these companies prefer retaining ownership and listing would dilute the ownership then the majority of these companies have not opted for listing hence prefer other options to raise funds. As already mentioned above, only twenty- three companies' have listed by the year end of twenty sixteen as they met the listing conditions. The nature of companies in Tanzania as explained above has its challenges when it comes to the collection of data for analysis. Listed companies' financial information is available as it is publishable, but data from unlisted companies is secrecy as it is not publishable hence becomes a challenge for research purpose.

1.5. Statement of the Research Problem

Capital structure studies are progressive. Initially, Modigliani and Miller (1958) introduced the concept, later followed by other different scholars who came up with further theories on the subject. However, an in-depth study of the previous literature reveals that the majority of the scholars on the subject studied capital structure determinants of companies in developed countries and less in developing countries (Suzan and Nico 2001: Achy 2009: Graham et al. 2010 and Tadele 2013). We also know that capital structure studies across time, in different countries, have underscored the influence of capital structure determinants on company leverages. Wald (1999) indicates growth potential as a determinant factor of the capital structure while Vivian (2005) study on French wine companies shows that determinants of capital structure are company size, asset structure, profitability, risk, growth, and non-debt tax shield and business age. Rajan and Zingales (1995) study indicated that variables such as tangibility, firm size, and market to book ratio (investment opportunities), ownership and control are the determinants of capital structure and these factors had a positive influence on the leverage of companies in these countries.

Other studies by different scholars on the subject reveal that capital structure determinants that affect company leverage in various countries include company age (Abhor 2008; Diamond, 1989; Murinde 2002) and size (Aryeetey 1994, Castanias 1983, Smith 1977 and Scott 1977; Kim &Sorenson 1986). Other studies reveal assets structures (Majluf 1984, Rajan 1996) and profitability (Myers 1984, Titman 1988, Rajan and Zingales 1995, Murinde 2004 and Olayinka (2011) as capital structure determinants. The empirical evidence by different scholars on what influences capital structure in developed countries also determinants also influence capital structure in developing countries (Diamond, 1989; Joseph, 1999; Rajan & Zingales, 1995 and Abor and Biekeppe, 2007).

Despite the empirical evidence on the capital structure determinants and the influence of these factors on company leverage in a global context, little is known about the influence of these factors on the leverage of Tanzanian companies as predicted by pecking order and trade- off Theories. This evidence of inadequate literature on the subject matter in Tanzania creates a research gap which motivates a study of this kind to fill it. The study is expected to add to the body of knowledge on what really influences capital structure choices among listed and unlisted company's Tanzanian companies.

Capital structure studies in Tanzania are few but a number of these studies available have not studied the relationship between capital structure determinants and leverage but studied the relationship between capital structure and company variables. Amani (2015) investigated the relationship between capital structure and firm's performance of non-financial corporations in listed in Dar Es Salaam Stock Exchange. Moses et al. (2016) studied only the financing alternatives for SACCOS and their impact on economic Performance and Tobias, Audi and Michael (2016) study investigated the determinants of bank capital structure only.

At the same time, studies that have tried to underscore various factors that influence company leverage in Tanzania did use a small number of companies as a sample representative of Tanzanian companies while there are more than 480 companies in Tanzania. Machogu and Bundala (2012)) studied the factors influencing capital structure of Tanzanian companies by using only a sample of eight listed companies. The use of such a small sample is not expected to produce robust results that can generalize the influence of profitability, age, size, liquidity and tangibility on leverages of Tanzanian companies and therefore a need to conduct a different study that can provide robust answers generated from a larger sample. Therefore, this kind of study that tries to underscore the study of the same subject matter by using a large sample of both listed and unlisted companies is expected to give robust results on the influence of selected capital structure variables on the leverage of Tanzanian companies as per Pecking order and Trade off Theories arguments on capital structure.

1.6. Research Objectives

Main Research objective

To examine the extent to which company liquidity, profitability, tangibility and, company size influences the leveraging of Tanzanian companies as suggested by Pecking Order and Trade off theory.

Specific Research Objectives
1. To establish the degree of leverage among listed and unlisted companies in Tanzania.
2. To examine the extent to which liquidity influences the leverage of Tanzanian companies as implied by the Pecking order theory and Trade off Theory.
3. To explore the extent to which profitability affects the leverage of Tanzanian companies suggested by the Pecking order and Trade-off theory.
4. As implied by pecking order and trade-off theory, examine the extent to which tangibility influences the leverage of Tanzanian companies.
5. To establish the extent to which company size influences leverage of Tanzanian companies as suggested by trade off theory and pecking order theory.

1.7. Research Questions

Main Research Question

To what extent company liquidity, profitability and tangibility and size influence the leverage of Tanzanian companies as implied by trade-off theory and pecking order theory?

Specific Research Question
1. What is the significance difference on leverage of among Tanzanian companies?

2. To what extent does liquidity influence the leverage of Tanzanian companies as implied by trade-off theory and the pecking order theory?
3. To what extent does profitability influence the leverage of Tanzanian companies implied by pecking order theory?
4. To what extent does tangibility influence the leverage of Tanzanian companies implied by trade-off theory and pecking order theory?
5. To what extent does company size influence the leverage of Tanzanian companies as implied by trade-off theory and the pecking order theory?

1.8. Significance of the study

By conducting this research, we expect some contributions to the academic and practitioner's world. The purpose of our study is not to come up with a new theory but to contribute to the literature on the capital structure by revealing the level of gearing of unlisted and listed companies in Tanzania and explains whether different capital structure determinants influence company leverage of Tanzanian companies. At the same time, inadequate studies on the subject matters from developing countries such as Tanzania do not give profound insights to scholars, academicians, and practitioners to understand and know whether capital structure determinants influence leverage measures.

This study will use data from Tanzanian companies for a longer duration of seven years (2007 -2014) which justifies the change of financing patterns of Tanzanian Companies. In this period the capital and financial market have deepened enough to allow companies to raise funds by using different sources such as stock listing and securing long-term debts from commercial banks. Within this period, for example, the commercial banks in Tanzania increased regarding numbers, and they came up with different financial products allowing companies to have access to loans funding.

Detailed analysis of the previous studies as revealed in the literature shows that debt to equity ratio and debt ratio was used as the measure of company leverage. However, these studies majored in developing countries and few studies in less developed countries. There are inadequate studies in Tanzania that have applied the same measures of leverage.

In the end, this study will add value to the body of knowledge and literature on capital structure determinants in more countries other than from the developed countries where capital structure determinants were initially tested. The study will add to the literature gap and will shed light on scholars and academicians on the subject matter.

This study is also essential, as it will entail the testing of applicability of the pecking order and trade off theories on capital structure determinants in a less developed country like Tanzania as most ideas have originated and tested in developed countries where the economic environment is different.

1.9. Scope and limitation of the Study

The study concentrated on the listed and Unlisted companies over the period beginning the year 2007 to the year 2014. However, not all companies were included in the study. All companies in the financial sector which include the banks, insurance companies and all companies providing financial services are excluded from the study. The study has not studied all standard capital structure determinants which are established by previous reviews, but it has limited itself to main four conventional determinant factors namely profitability, tangibility, size and liquidity. The selection of the study variables is based on the researcher preferences to use only quantifiable variables and excluding the qualitative variables.

1.10. Organization of the Report

This research paper comprises five chapters including this chapter. Chapter one discusses the historical background to the research problem, research objectives, and research questions and the significance of the study as well. Chapter two is the literature of the study that gives the background on the critical issues of Capital structure, capital structure theories, capital structure determinants, empirical findings and the research gap. Chapter 3 discusses the conceptual framework and the research methodology. Chapter 4 presents the research findings of the study, and finally, chapter 5 gives the conclusions and recommendations of the study.

CHAPTER TWO

LITERATURE REVIEW

2.1. Introduction

This chapter discusses the capital structure theoretical foundation. The section will address the fundamental issues related to capital structure and developed theories over time. The chapter also underscores pieces of evidence from past literature on factors that can influence the leverage of companies and reasons as to why some of the determinants elements are used in this specific study. The second part of the discussion shows the surveys of empirical evidence on capital structure theories and determinants that have been undertaken across different countries in the world.

2.2. Capital Structure definition, relevance and measurement

The first scholars to study and publish on capital structure were Modigliani and Miller (1958). This first attempt of study laid a solid foundation for other scholars to continue exploring in depth about this concept. According to Weston and Bringham (1978) businesses can finance business organization by using equity stock, preference shares and long-term debts. The fundamental issue with this definition is on the source of financing where there is a precise identification of capital structure which includes long-term debt, preference shares, ordinary shares, reserves, and surplus. Raymond (1979) argues about the importance of planning capital structure in consideration of shareholders interest, company financial requirements and benefits of other groups (creditors, customers, etc.) while maximizing the long-term market value per share.

The argument by Raymond (1979) on shareholders' interest is that when a company raises more funds by way of equity, there is a high possibility of diluting the shareholders controlling power. The raising of funds through more debts increases risks and hence greater likelihood for insolvency. The financial needs of the company also determine whether the company should continue raising funds through debts or equity. The company cannot keep borrowing further funds if it has already met its financial requirements otherwise the unused funds could increase unnecessary costs to the organization. Myers (2001) and Niu (2008) show the combination of different sources of funds which represent the capital structure of the company. This definition emphasizes the nature of the source of finance. Significant contents of capital structure are equity and debts (short term or long- term debts), while equity is composed of preferred shares, preference shares, and retained earnings. Jong and Koedijk (2006) argue that capital structure deals with how companies handle their financing activities. This means how they make choices between the use of equity or use of debts.

The use of debts or equity to finance business organization, whether the short-term or long-term source of finance is essential for business continuity or survival. Onaolapo and Kajola (2010) suggest that companies should try to use different sources of financing their business organization and should avoid the inappropriate combination of various sources of finance. The use of varying mix of capital, however, it depends a lot on some factors including the operating business environment. All of the above capital structure definitions given by different authors have shared characteristics as well as minor differences. Firstly, they all provide the nature or components of capital structure that it is comprised of debts and equity instrument. Secondly, they give the basis for how each business can opt to finance its business activities either using debt or equity instruments.

Various scholars have discussed the relevancy of this concept to the business organization. Yona (2011) argues that Capital structure gives a guide to managers on how to approach all investment decisions. In evaluating investment projects, the use of various methods of investment appraisal and financing method consideration is essential. Raising funds through debts, can lead to high risk, for example, to finance an investment project in case the project is unable to generate enough cash flow to liquidate the financial obligations. However, when raising funds through the issue of shares, there is the possibility of diluting ownership power and jeopardizing shareholders interest. Further division of capital structure as stated by Mostafa and Borgwanda (2014) includes internal funds which are represented by retained earnings and external financing. This refers to the issue of equity or debt instruments. Where company's assets are highly financed by debts, the company is termed to be highly geared or highly levered. Capital structure as a terminology is much related to finance structure and financial gearing

2.2.1 Modigliani Miller Arguments

Modigliani and Miller arguments (1958) considers number of assumptions that do not affect the value of the firm. Therefore, in raising finances, a perfect market is assumed with assumptions that there is an expectation that managers can use any sources of finances without undermining shareholders interest and firms' value. In this kind of market there is a free flow of information and no information costs. They further argue that in a perfect market there is divisibility of shares, no transaction costs such as flotation costs and there is rationality of decisions by participants as they try maximizing profits or minimize their losses. Further assumptions of the perfect world are that companies can only issue two types of financing instrument namely, equity and debt with no risk, both insider and outsider have no information asymmetry, and no different kinds of threats exist. However, under this assumption, Modigliani and Miller do not suggest for an optimal structure which companies should adopt.

In the real world, all conditions of the perfect world explained they don't exist in the modern world. Empirical evidence shows the non-existence of an ideal world (perfect world). In the imperfect world companies not performing well might experience bankruptcy costs, taxes have to be paid by companies doing business and transaction costs do exists in any business transaction. In theory, the perfect world exists but in reality, it cannot. In fact, such an ideal world has never existed as Bringham, and Capenski (1996) indicate that all the conditions assumed not to exist they are the reality of life in the business organization.

Denying these critical factors couldn't go so far, and therefore Modigliani and Miller (1963) further revised their irrelevance theory by introducing corporate taxes as a condition in the imperfect market. Modigliani and Miller Proposition II incorporated the tax benefit which companies receive when they do debt financing. Companies that issue debt instruments have the advantage of paying fewer taxes as the interest on debts is allowable as tax expenses. Therefore, it is argued that debt financing relative to equity financing is a preferred choice for an organization financing even though over time as companies continue borrowing, they tend to default on interest rates payments, leading to incurrence of bankruptcy costs.

Further research studies by Myers and Majluf (1984) which contravened Modigliani and Miller (1958) with propositions that market perfections conditions are not rare to find and therefore company leverage affects the firm valuation. The findings proved that the propositions of global perfect market conditions do not hold water. In summary, we can conclude that the MM1 propositions emphasized that company value cannot be influenced by the use of equity or debt financing. This means that the existence of market imperfections is more of a realistic situation than existence of the perfect world.

Over time Modigliani and Miller (1963) relaxed the original conditions and introduced new assumptions in their theory. MM Proposition II was more of the relaxation of the previous conditions to the imperfection of the market and hence by incorporating taxes which lead to the conclusion that under the imperfect world value of the firm can be affected by its capital structure.The assumptions of this theory laid the foundation of the development of new approaches as the result of relaxation of the premises and critiques laid down by modern scholars. The M1 and M2 assumptions relaxation have led to the development of new theories on capital structure which we discuss below. These theories are the Trade-off theory (Scott

1977, Kim 1978) (Kraus & Litzenberger (1973), Miller (1977), Pecking order (Myers & Majluf1984) and Agency costs (Ross 1977). These theories diverged from the assumptions of the perfect world by relaxing the market perfection conditions and tried to offer alternative explanations on how managers can approach the financing decisions of their organizations.

In summary we can conclude that the proposition 1 of Modigliani and Miller emphasized that the value of the firm is not influenced by its capital structure (whether issuing debt or equity) but it assumed the existence of the perfect world which in reality it does not exists. Proposition II was more of the relaxation that allowed the imperfection of the market by incorporating taxes which then lead to influence the capital structure of the firm. The assumptions of these theory laid the foundation of development of new capital structure as the result of relaxation of the assumptions and critiques laid down by new scholars on the capital structure subject. Further theories emerged later that have diverged from the assumptions of the perfect world by relaxing the market perfection conditions and tried to offer alternative explanations on capital structure decisions. These theories include the Static Trade off theory (Myers and Majluf,1984), Pecking order theory (Myers and Majluf,1984), Agency Cost Theory (Ross 1976) and capital structure organizational life stage theory (Addizes, 1979, Frielinhaus et al 2005).

2.3.2. Static Tradeoff Theory

The static trade-off theory was first derived from the work of Myers (1984). It is a prominent theory which ignores the existence of perfect world assumptions as per Modigliani and Miller (1958). The static trade-off theory emphasizes on the need for the companies to have target capital structure choice of using either from internal sources or external sources. The approach assumes that companies operate in a market full of uncertainties and risks, however, they are capable of selecting their target capital structure in consideration of other factors such as the benefits derived from balancing the gains from interest payment and cost of issuing debts (Johanzeb et al. 2014).

To achieve a target capital structure, the theory incorporated the tax shield benefit which companies enjoy when they opt to finance their business operations by using debts. The tax shield benefit encourages companies to use debts to seek to finance the business organization (Miller, 1998) only where bankruptcy costs are low or non-existent. At the same time, (Majluf and Majluf, 1984) shows that the theory puts emphasize on balancing the bankruptcy costs with the level of debts a company opts to take. The Static Trade-off theory does not suggest a standard target but indicates for optimal debt-equity ratio or a range for this ratio that minimizes a firm's average cost. Myers (1984) does not support Miller's propositions on the basis that there are higher possibilities that; the increase in the level of debts increases the bankruptcy costs. This places an upper limit on the amount of debt that should be present in a company capital structure.

Myers (2001) further contends for the existence of high debt ratios in more profitable companies as this gives advantages to companies to enjoy tax shield benefits, which implies that such companies use more debts. This is not a reality because highly profitable companies usually tend to have less debt. According to Skyam (1999) pecking order theory has much more explanatory power than the trade- off theory which emphasizes on having target capital structure. Graham and Havey (2001) study that shows that companies could have target capital structure. Bancel & Mitttoo (2004) suggest that the use of optimal capital structure was 75% of all surveyed firms across number of companies in European countries, while Brouneni, de- Jong and Koedilk (2006) indicates that majority of large firms in Netherlands, UK, France, and Germany also maintained a target capital structure.

Static Trade-off theory further postulates that in early stage of company life, companies cannot afford to use debts as their bankruptcy costs are likely to be high and have the low capability of generating profits. Frielinghaus et al. (2005) findings in South Africa concluded that companies in infancy, go-go and adolescence stages cannot afford to use debt, as their bankruptcy costs are high and their earnings are too low to use tax benefit and increasing interest payments. However, at the end of the company lifecycle, when companies are likely to have much lower profits then debt use becomes a preference (Frielinghaus, 2005). In summary, the trade-off theory would suggest the little- high -low use of debt by companies across the life cycle, supporting the postulates of the life cycle theory.

2.3.3. Pecking Order Theory

This theory is a long-term theory which originated first from Donaldson's (1961) studies but never gained academic attention until Myers (1984) postulated its significant underlying assumptions. The assumptions are based on the hierarchical order of funding business operations first beginning with retained earnings, as it is considered as the cheapest source, then followed by equity and finally using debt instruments.

The critical issue addressed by this theory is the priority on using debt and internal sources of capital. The pecking model emphasizes more on optimal capital structure based on a combination of long-term funds and ignoring entirely short-term funds. According to this theory, companies follow a particular order in financing their businesses which emphasize on an optimal priority of hierarchical of raising of funds. This order follows a specific order starting with the use of internal equity (which includes capital and retained earnings) followed by application of debts. This is because internal equity is cheaper as compared to external financing through debt use since debt always attracts interest. Furthermore, the pecking order is a capital structure theory which negates the postulates of the organizational life cycle and trade-off theory. The pecking order follows a hierarchy of financing and suggests a high -low -high pattern of leverage across the entire lifetime stages. (Paula et al. 2014).

According to Frank and Goyal (2003) mature companies support the relevancy of the pecking order theory. Mature companies are considered to have gained a reputation over years which gives the opportunity to secure debts from different lenders easily. Companies at initial stages of their formation, however, have the problem of meeting conditions necessary to access equity funding. In summary, we can say the pecking order suggests that company age and capital structure are positively associated for at least two stages, namely at the initial stage and maturity stage of the company.

According to Myers and Majluf (1984) companies prefer internally generated sources to fund the business operation because supporting additional equity is expensive as compared to retained earnings. This hierarchy implies that profitable companies would have sufficient internally generated funds, hence use few debts as compared to unprofitable companies that employ more debts.

Myers (1984) assumes that there are no corporate taxes and the company is making a profit throughout its lifetime. However, there are only a few countries in the world today where there are no corporate taxes, and even if corporate taxes did not exist, the world is full of market imperfections therefore making it harder for this theory to hold water. Changes in economic conditions are likely to affect the profitability of companies such that they are not able to raise funds by using their retained earnings. Many authors have different arguments and assumptions about the pecking order. In general, the hypothesis is an explicit model of the financing decisions order.

The use of the internal source of finance (equity) followed by application of external claims (debts) was also propagated by Ross (1977. The reason for this argument is that internal equity is the most preferable as it is the cheapest source of finance. Shyam & Myers (1999) argues that the pecking order theory is the best theory to adopt as it helps to predict the option of companies when it comes to choosing the method of financing their business operations. Ye Zhang (2010) argue that although there are more opponent voices, pecking order theory is still regarded as the light reflection to the present world. Stewart (2001), in challenging this theory, argued about its inadequacy to indicate what are the incentives for managers preferring to raise funds through internal sources.

In summary, the pecking order emphasizes the optimal priority of hierarchical raising of funds. Allen (1993) studied found that pecking order theory was more relevant as companies' operations used first the retained earnings followed by external funding. The study also reveals for existence of positive significant relationship between profitability and leverage. Fama and French (1988) findings show that profitability and company capital structure are negatively correlated. The observations of company's balance sheet by Myers (1984) also indicated that the structuring of company balance sheet tend to follow the pecking order assumption whereby use of the external source is thought as the last option after exhausting the internal sources.

Further interpretation and understanding of this theory by modern scholars are other [40] issues to look into it. Lemmon et al (2008) study gave new insights on understanding the pecking order which led them to adopt a concept of debt capacity suggesting that companies can only consider equity issue once equity financing when debt financing is not feasible. This helps to limit the amount of capital structure within the pecking order and to limit the use of equity. This interpretation has not easily been accepted in the academic literature. Leary and Roberts (2010) critiques on Lemmon, Robert, and Zender (2008) suggested for flexibility of the pecking order which could allow for flexibility in the capital structure. They believed that when company debt capacities are adjusted, it could allow improving their capital structure. Graham and Heavy (2001) concluded that managers seek a target debt-equity ratio not to minimize a firm weighted average cost of capital but rather to keep financial flexibility in the context of pecking order theory.

2.3.4. Organizational life stage theory

The theory originates from the assumptions that all business has a life cycle and at each stage of company life cycle business can raise funds differently. The arguments on this theory are on the life stages of the organizations. Adzizes (1979) argues that the financing at each phase of the organization life cycle will differ from one step to another. At the early stage of conceiving the business idea, there is no capital structure as compared to further stages. While at infancy stage the company cash flow is negative. At additional stages when investment requires more money; the company needs more external financing. At adolescence stage, there is the high need for growth and profits. At this juncture, the introduction of private equity investors and use of IPO could generate funds to sustain growth. At a go-go stage; the company is growing, and it will need to increase its sales and the sphere of influence and therefore more need for external financing. Damodaran (2001) suggests that expanding and high growth companies would prefer to finance themselves with equity while maturing companies would use more debts for capital financing. Opler and Titman (2001) argue that businesses at the mature stage should use more debts to finance assets in place and more equity to fund business growth therefore progressively continuing to use more debt in the funding their capital structure mix. In support of this argument, Frielingahus et al. (2005) summarized the life stage theory into ten steps starting from courtship, infancy, go-go, adolescence, prime, stable aristocracy, recrimination, bureaucracy and death. In each of these stages, methods of capital financing will differ. Panigraph (2011) also support this theory that the life cycle of the company influences the company capital structure.

2.4. Capital Structure Theories link with Company Leverage

In this section, the discussion is on capital structure theories predictions as related to the factors which influence company leverage. However, the debate will only adopt the prominent capital structure theories. These theories are assumed to have a relationship with the selected capital structure and have relationship with company leverage.

Table 2.1 Predicted Sign of Relationship between Variables and Capital structure Theories

Variable	Pecking Order Theory	Static Trade off Theory
Profitability	-	+
Liquidity	-	+
Tangibility	+	+
Size	-	

Source: Researcher 2017

According to Myers and Majluf (1984) the choice of financing method used, whether internal or external sources, mostly depends on the profitability of companies. Companies with higher profits would prefer using more debts while unprofitable companies are limited debt use as lenders might have less confidence with such companies. Myers further argued that profitable companies would finance their operations from external sources and hence use fewer debts. Caglayan and Sak (2010) study found that profitability of banks studied were negatively correlated to book leverage which is consistent to the prediction of the pecking order.

The results are not contrary to the prediction of the pecking order theory. Hans-Suck (2005) also indicate that a negative significant relationship exists between leverage and profitability in their study. According to Booth, et al (2001) profitability and leverage are negatively correlated. The study by Frank and Goyal (2002) supports these findings and confirms the importance of the pecking order. However, Johansen et al. (1992) indicate that trade-off theory prediction has significance in their findings as the study reveals a significant impact of profitability on leverage.

Shyam Sunder and Myers 1999, Mackay and Philips (2001) studies also confirmed that profitability has significant impacts on leverage confirming the prediction of the trade-off theory. These predictions are based on the fact that as companies generate more profits and more cash, managers tend to relax and misuse the funds therefore increasing the likelihood of companies incurring cash shortages and consequently turning back to debt option to resolve the problem. Previous studies by Long and Maltzi (1985) suggest that profitability and leverage are positively correlated hence supporting the trade-off theories arguments. On the other side there is assumed a positive relationship between tangibility and leverage which is in conformity to Trade-off theory predictions. Companies with high level of tangibility, use the assets as collateral hence have easy to access more debts (Myers and Majluf 1984).

The study findings by Frank and Goyal (2006) reveal that tangibility and company leverage are positively related confirming the postulates laid down under pecking order theory. Similar results that show same relationship between these two variables are the studies by Shah and Khan (2007), Gaud et al. (2003) study findings reveal that tangibility and leverage are positively associated which is in conformity to the claimed assumptions of the prominent trade off theory.

However, the prediction of the pecking order theory relationship between tangibility and leverages have a negative correlation. More assets reduce the information asymmetry level hence leading to cheaper equity (Harris and Ravis 1991). According to Cornell et al. (1996), study findings reveal that tangibility and debt ratios are negatively correlated, contrary to trade off theory predictions. According to De Angelo and Masulis (1980), tangibility is negatively correlated with leverage. Pandey (2001) was not different from the previous findings on negativism association between asset tangibility and leverage. These findings contradicted the prediction of the trade-off theory.

According to Titman and Wessels (1988) study findings company size and leverage are positively related. These findings are supported by the predictions of trade-off theory and previous studies. At the same time, Gaud (2006) study findings indicate the support of the tradeoff theory and show that size is positively correlated to financial structure emphasizing that large companies easily access financial services and capital markets. Contrary to the previous study on the service industry, Gill et al. (2009) indicate that capital structure and size are negatively related suggesting that company leverage is not influenced by company size. However, it is evident that company size affects the leverage whether it is a more significant or small company because companies with more significant size tend to pay their debts quickly than smaller ones; lenders are likely to give more debts to larger companies. The prediction of the Pecking order is contrary to these findings. According to Olllala, (2016) companies with larger size are likely to raise funds through equity. The pecking order also assumes that companies which have a larger amount of cash and other liquid assets are the base for building up enough cash reserves which can be available for use instead of using debt.

Organization life cycle theory suggests that company age is positively related to company leverage. According to Myers (2001) at commencement stage of business, companies use debts as means for funding their operations due to inadequate profits but later use the debts as they get matured since are now capable of generating higher profits. In decline stage they normally use more debts because of the decline in profits. Nico and Van Hulle

(2010) suggest that older companies have a long-term track record and strong reputation which leads to a better relationship with lenders hence having access to debts at the low cost of debt. Therefore, with this theory, it is assumed that company age and leverage of Companies are positively related. Studies confirming this positivism relationship is many as well as those who predict negative relationship.

2.5. Summary of Theories, Assumptions, conclusion, and Relevance

The discussed capital structure theories above have highlighted their underlying assumptions and their predictions on the relationship to company leverage underlying the basis for their applicability and relevance in the business world. The theories emphasize on compliance to this assumption which represents the optimal financing strategy. Pecking order theory, for example, gives the understanding that companies making higher profits are capable of generating adequate funding to finance their activities through retained earnings and they may not take more debts (Myers, 1984). It also assumes the preference hierarchy of a company in financing its investment. However, less profitable companies cannot have adequate retained earnings hence compelled to take on more debts to finance their activities. The model as confirmed by previous studies predicts for various relationships between various predictors (tangibility, profitability, liquidity, size) and leverage. Myers and Majluf (1984) support the negative correlation between profitability and leverage.

Furthermore, in arguments of (POT) always liquidity will be negative correlated to leverage and it supports positive relationship between size of the company and its leverage. The static trade-off theory assumption assumes that companies reach their debt capacity by fixing their desired target by management and it concludes for a mixed relationship between company leverage and size, profitability, liquidity, and tangibility. The theory supports positivism between profitability and leverage ratio. Prediction of Tradeoff Theory (TOT) confirms the positivism relationship between size and leverage. This prediction gives relevance in such a way that managers can have the freedom to make choices on how best they can finance business activities on behalf of business owners after considering other factors that can influence the selection of financing method.

2.6. Empirical Literature

The literature review discusses the justification of selecting the variables that have been used in this study and we also give the empirical evidences from various global studies.

2.6.1. Justification on Selection of Capital structure determinants

In this section, we discuss the justification of selecting capital structure determinants and how it has been applied in the Tanzanian case. There are many types of capital structure determinants that have been discussed in the literature and used in various studies in the global arena. However, the empirical research discussed in the following section covers only the standard capital structures determinants that are incorporated in the conceptual model of the study. Capital structure determinants selected for this study include company size, profitability, tangibility, and liquidity. The reasons as to why these factors are selected are because of the quantitative characteristic of these variables.

An explanatory study of this nature requires the use of quantitative data to analyze the data derived from financial statements and therefore a need to exclude capital structure determinants that use the qualitative information to interpret them. The empirical literature excludes some standard capital structure determinants with qualitative characteristics. These include entrepreneurship background (Briozzo and Vigier 2009), Agency problems (Wu, Song and Zeng 2008), external shocks, managerial ownership, family involvement, demand and supply of debt fund, shareholders interest, company uniqueness, country-specific factors, industry classification and business orientation. (Titman 1988: Fatma and Media 2009: Booth 2001). Studying the determinant factors based on qualitative data in Tanzania is also an area which has not been exploited and a recommendation for another study.

2.6.2. Determinants of capital structure

The literature on capital structure across the globe has revealed a variety of determinant factors which are portable across the whole world except for few exceptions. Titman (1988) portrayed that capital structure of companies is influenced by such factors as company uniqueness, company size, earnings volatility and growth. Standard variables which are portable include company size, age, asset structure and, profitability (Sheridan 1988 and Diamond, 1989). In their findings, Michael (1989) and Joseph, (1999) studies also confirm the similar type of relationship. According to Drobetz and Fix (2003) asset tangibility is associated with leverage and profitability is negative related to leverage. These findings are similar to other previous (Diamond, 1989; Joseph,1999; Rajan & Zingales, 1995 and Abor and Biekeppe, 2007) which also indicate existence that tangibility is negatively related to company leverage.

Graham (2000) on the cross-sectional study of 3500 Unquoted SME companies in the United Kingdom revealed that Capital structure variables indicated various relationships. Asset structure and company size were positively related to long-term debt ratios, age had the negative correlation with long-term debt ratio while profitability, asset structure, company size was negatively correlated to short-term debt ratio. Profitability also did not affect long-term debts. The study by Booth et al (2001) on ten countries (Pakistan, Thailand, Korea, Brazil, Mexico, Zimbabwe) covering the period between 1980 and 1990 found that factors influencing leverage of these countries were the same. The study by Ozkan (2001) on 390 UK Companies during the 1984-1996 period indicate that companies have a long run target leverage ratio and company size has limited impact on the capital structure. Study on capital structure in the UK by Ozkan (2001) underscored the relationship that exists between profitability, tangibility and liquidity, profitability found that these variables were positively related to leverage. The study by Huang and Song (2002) investigated 1000 companies china for a period between 1994 and 2000. Study findings show that company size and tangibility is positively related to firms leverage while profitability was negatively correlated to leverage. Another study by Cassar and Holmes (2003) findings indicate that profitability is positively related to leverage.

Chen (2004) examined the capital structure of Chinese listed companies and concluded that specific variables of company characteristics that explain the subject in modern countries (Western nations) also influence leverage of Chinese companies' capital despite of the profound country-specific differences existing in these countries. These findings shed light on scholars that the same factors which explain what influences the leverage companies in China could be relevant in Tanzania. Voulgaris et al. (2004) study in Greece found that profitability was a significant determinant of financing decision in large companies although Nakaumira and Juca (2005) study concluded that profitability was negatively correlated to leverage which is consistent to pecking order postulates. In Nepal context, Baral (2004) investigated 40 listed companies for period 2003. Study findings indicate existence of positive significant impact of size on leverage although business risks and dividend payout ratio have an insignificant relationship with company leverage. Rajan and Zingales (2005) study of G-7 Countries (USA, Germany, Japan, France, Italy, U.K and Canada) observed that tangibility, sales, and profitability influenced company leverage.

Gaud et al. (2005) examined the relationship between firm specific factors and company leverage of 104 Swiss listed companies between years 1991 and 2000 using a dynamic panel framework. The study findings reveal a positive correlation between tangibility, size, and leverage while profitability was negatively correlated. The study by Gajural (2005) investigated the factors influencing company leverage in Nepalese of both listed and the unlisted companies in the period between the year 1992 and 2004. They showed a negative association existed between size and leverage that but asset structure and size are positively associated to leverage. Kalu Ojah and Justo Manrique (2005) study on the determinant of corporate debt structures highlights some these factors which affect debt financing. They argue that the determinant of business capital debt structure in an environment where companies have access to full complements of public and private debts may differ from those in an atmosphere where companies' access is restricted only to private debts. A further finding of their study reveals a positive correlation between use of debts and company size but the existence of a negative association between use of debts and companies' creditworthiness. At the same time, they found the likelihood of using non-bank private debts is positively related to company size, growth potential, relative company size and degree of leverage.

Furthermore, Song (2005) investigates the factors which have a significant relationship on the leverage of 6,000 Swedish companies for years beginning 1992 to 2000. The study indicate that company leverage is positively related to company specific factors namely tangibility, profitability and income variability but company uniqueness had negative relationship with company leverage. Hysung et al. (2006) studied the capital structure dynamics of Korean companies and used unbalanced panel data for the period between 1985 and 2002 aimed at identifying the factors that influence company leverage. The results of the findings reveal that Korean specific factors namely company size, profitability and growth opportunity had a positive influence on company leverage

Joshua (2007) cross-sectional study in Ghana based on a sample of 160 SMEs used correlation and regression model. The study findings reveal that company size is positively related to debt ratios which was consistent with life-cycle theory. Further findings show that tangibility is also positively related to long term debt ratio. The study results show that collateral plays a significant role for SME to access to long-term debt finance. The study also found the negative association between asset structure and short-term debt ratio which indicated that companies in Ghana tried to finance their fixed assets with long-term debts and their current assets with short-term debts.

This Jean (2008) studied 410 French wine companies during the year 2000-2004 led to conclude that capital structure determinant in the wine industry is very similar to other sectors. The studies also revealed that Pecking order theory seemed to explain leverage than other models like the trade-off theory. In the same agenda examining the capital structure, In the environment of Pakistan Waliullah and Nishat (2008) investigated 533 non- financial listed companies. The study adopted the autoregressive distributed lag (ARDL) methodology. Results reveal that the existence of a positive relationship between growth opportunities, Size and leverage. However, the study showed that profitability and liquidity were negatively related. Another study by Daskalakis and Psillaki (2008) investigated the capital structure of-quoted SMEs in France and Greece by applying panel data method to sample of SMEs for period 1998-2002. The study assessed the influence of capital structure determinants influences the leverage of companies. Study findings reveal the existence of negative relationship between profitability and tangibility but a firm size having a positive association with leverage ratios.

Fitmi and Media (2009) studied firm characteristics and their influence on capital structure among Macedonia listed and unlisted firms for period 2005-2009. The study found that Macedonian firms preferred to have access to equity financing simply because of the price of stocks being lower. In another study, Frank and Goyal (2009) investigates the extent to which the US-listed companies for the years between 1990 and 2003 company specific factors are related to leverage such as size, tangibility, how firm size and tangibility. The study findings revealed a positive association between firm size, tangibility and market ratio and company leverage.

Raflu and Obafemi (2009) studied 50 non-financial quoted Nigerian companies from the year 1990 to 2004 and used the pooled ordinary least squares (OLS) model, Random Effect Model and Fixed Effect Model (FEM) to analyze the data. Research findings indicate that profitability is positively correlated with short-term debt but negatively related to long-term debt. Generally, this study also reported that Nigerian companies depended so much on debts in funding their business operations

The study of Qui and La (2010) in Australia underscored how firm characteristics influence company leverage choices. The result findings reveal that asset tangibility, growth prospects, business risks and profitability are significant to leverage but company size was negatively related to debt ratio. Furthermore, Ye Zhang (2010) investigated the factors which affect the company leverage of 220 SME companies in Britain manufacturing industries majority of them being unlisted companies. Based on regression model found that tangibility, size and company profitability was significantly related to debt ratio.

Sulgana et al. (2010) study on companies in India based on prowess data of 891 different companies used a partial adjustment model to conclude that tangibility, size profitability and leverage are negatively associated. Emilio (2010) examined the capital structure 1100 Hungarian companies between the year 1992 and 1996. The study results show that profitability, size and tangibility, and size was positively correlated to company leverage. In the context of Iran environment, Mahdi et al. (2010) examined the influence of profitability on firms leverage, and the results suggest that profitability is negatively correlated to capital structure.

Mishira (2011) investigated the extent to which capital structure determinants influenced the leverage of Indian Public-sector undertakings, and the results indicated that tangibility, profitability, tax, growth, and asset has significant impact on leverage but size found no significant related to leverage. Furthermore, in the Nigerian context, Akinlo and Obafemi (2011) examined the relationship of firm's characteristics of property companies and found a significant positive correlation between company size, asset tangibility, and leverage but profitability was negatively related to total debt ratio. Furthermore, Velnampy and Niresh (2012) examined Srilanka companies for eight years between 2002 and 2009 finding out whether profitability of companies influences company leverage. Results findings indicate that profitability was negatively correlated to company leverage. In their survey of financial services in China, Thian and Xian Jiao (2012) examined the influence firm specific factors on company leverages over the years 2005 to 2009. Study findings show that company size, profitability, earnings volatility and non-circulating shares are positively related

In another study, Pinkova (2012) studied the determinants influencing the company leverage in the automotive industry in the Czech Republic. The study investigated 129 companies to cover a period from 2006 t0 2010. The study adopted variance, correlation, and regression analysis to analyze the data. The findings reveal that tangibility, profitability, liquidity, and size appear to have a significant relationship with leverage but growth is not a statistically related to company leverage. These findings are opposite to static trade-off theory postulates and the arguments of the pecking order theory.

The study by Md Yusuf et al. (2013) of electrical and electronic sector listed companies show that profitability, size, tangibility is positively related to company leverage consistency to findings of other previous studies and the postulates of the trade-off theory. Further findings show that liquidity has a negative relationship to leverage which confirms the pecking order postulates. Tekele (2013) studied what impacts the leverage of private firms manufacturing in Ethiopia. Ordinary square multiple regression model was applied to analyze sample data of 10 selected manufacturing firms. The research suggests for a positive association between company size, profitability, tangibility and long-term debt ratio of assets are found to liquidity has a strong significant effect on the short-term debt. Research findings further show that majority of Ethiopian companies' finance their assets using short-term debts such as bank overdraft and trade creditors while large firm uses more extended loans than small firms. Furthermore, Ishaya et al. (2013) studied Nigerian chemical and paint companies' sector between years 2005 and 2009. The study revealed for the Nigerian chemical and paint sector, profitability tangibility has negative relationship to leverage, but these findings were inconsistent to the propositions of both Trade off and pecking order theories.

Another scholar research (Bayeh (2013) analyzed how company size and profitability could influence the leverage of Insurance companies in Ethiopia. The study reveals that size did not have any impact on capital structure decisions but indicated existence that profitability has significant impact on leverage. The study of 19,000 Brazilian Companies by De Forte, Barros, and Nakamura (2013) reveal that much significant relationship exists between size and leverage which is consistent with pecking order arguments. Results shows that small companies can efficiently use external sources after using internal sources (retained earnings). The results also show a significant negative impact of profitability on leverage. At the same time size and leverage are positively related to leverage, this meant that larger companies could easily access external funds. Serbian, Ksenja and Emma (2013) modeled leverage as the function of company-specific factors namely cash gap, profitability, and tangibility. The study results reveal that profitability, liquidity and cash gap was negatively associated with company leverage but profitability and income volatility were positively related to leverage consistently to previous findings and pecking order theory postulates.

Songul K (2014) studied manufacturing companies in Turkey and results show that tangibility and profitability and asset structure had more significant effects more than other capital structure determinant variables on leverage in all manufacturing sectors. Other studies by Awan and Amin (2014) studied the leverage of 68 textile firms of Pakistan listed companies for years between 2006 and 2012. They also studied which type of capital structure was more prevalent in the sector. The results reveal that all factors studied, tangibility, profitability, liquidity and size do have significant influence on total leverage and long-term leverage. Furthermore, Ab Wahab and Ramli (2014) study on 13 Malaysian listed companies between 1997 and 2009 showed that size and tangibility do have association with corporate financing, but liquidity is negatively related to leverage. In the same year in India, Handoo and Sharma (2014) investigated 870 companies and found capital structure determinants was significantly related to leverage as findings indicated that profitability, size, and tangibility were positively correlated to leverage.

Turki (2014) studied the extent to which companies' leverage is influenced by different company characteristics in Saudi Arabia. The study covered the period between the year 2010 and 2014 and adopted a cross-sectional pool data methodology. The findings suggest that tangibility of assets, risks, profitability and company leverage are negative related but there was a positive relationship between size and capital structure. Furthermore, in the global arena, there are other studies in the same year that shed light on the subject. Shrabanti (2014) investigated the 37 Indian steel companies with the main objective of exploring if there were specific factors that correlate to leverage of these companies. Research findings reveal profitability and business risk are negatively correlated with minimal effect on company leverage, but the size and company growth were positively related with leverage. Zubairi and Farooq (2014) study of listed companies in Pakistan for the years between 2000 and 2010 show that the risk-free interest rates, profitability, size of the firm, liquidity and tangibility of assets are positively related to leverage. Another study by Thippayana

(2014) examined 144 companies in Thailand for period between year 2000 and 2011. Study findings reveal that a significant relationship exists between size, profitability and company leverage.

Nelson et al. (2015) studied the stock listed market non-financial firms in Portugal to analyze the relationship between tangibility, profitability, size and company leverage. Their findings reveal for existence of a positive correlation between profitability and leverage but profitability and size were negative associated with debt ratios. Hussein et al. (2015) studied the capital structure of 450 Malaysian listed companies in Malaysian Food processing between 2003-2012 and employed the Pearson correlation coefficient and multiple linear regression. The study aimed to investigate whether profitability, asset tangibility, size, and liquidity influenced company to leverage. The findings reveal that profitability, size, tangibility is negatively associated with total debt ratio though significant tangibility was positively correlated to debt ratio. Mawih et al. (2015) investigated the extent to which tangibility, profitability influenced company leverage of Oman Companies for the years between 2008 and 2012. The study results show that tangibility and leverage are positively related but profitability was negatively related to leverage.

The demand and supply of debt funds determine the debt structure of the company. It is also evident that adequate resources or shortage of funds can influence the debt structure of a company. However, the cost of information gathering and monitoring costs on borrowers of different types of debts, mitigation information asymmetry, and efficiency liquidation, can impact the optimal debt structure (Jensen and Meckling, 1976: Rajan 1992). Rajan, however, acknowledges that short-term borrowings can expose a company to excessive liquidation. While debts are significant ingredients of capital structures, various factors influence the use of debts by companies.

Masoud (2014) examines the determinants which cause firms to choose equity over a debt of eight Libyan firms listed in the stock exchange over the period 2008 to 2013. He observes that high price-earnings ratios and high-interest rates reduce the cost of equity finance which causes firms to choose equity over debt. Nguyen and Dang (2016) established that time frame between long-term and short-term sources of finance could influence the choice of method on how to finance business operation. This means companies can opt for short- term or long- term sources of finance to fund their investments. Some companies may choose for debts in the long run or equity financing.

2.7. Research Gap

Based on discussion and empirical evidence above, it is evident that there is inadequate literature to support the study on capital structure in Tanzania thus a research gap to address. The insufficient studies on the subject matter do not reveal evidence on what influences Tanzanian companies to leverage neither explain the arguments of capital structure theories as confirmed by various capital structure determinants. The few studies that are available on capital structure are on listed companies and not for unlisted companies. At the same time, combined studies on the capital structure of both listed and unlisted companies in Tanzania are inadequate which create a research gap. Booth et al. (2010) study used only one country (Zimbabwe) to represent all developing countries in Africa. This situation has created a shallow body of knowledge in the subject matter.

By studying the previous literature in Tanzania on capital structure, it shows that these studies used a small sample to analyze their research data. Findings by Machogu (2012) study Tanzanian listed companies using a small sample of only eight listed companies in Tanzania. The use of a smaller sample is inadequate to give proper results hence a need for this type of research to fill the gap and provide empirical evidence by exploring the case of both listed and unlisted Tanzanian companies while using a larger sample.

At the same time, previous studies in Tanzania used a small sample of companies to analyze or establish whether capital structure determinants have any linkage with company leverage. Lastly, studying capital structure determinants in multiple sectors is likely to provide new insight into the subject matter as compared to previous studies which involved few companies operating in few economic areas.

2.8. Key Issue, lessons learned and Conclusions

This chapter has discussed the underlying epistemology of the capital structures theories that have been developed by different scholars over the years. Further discussions have been on determinants factors of capital structures and their influence on the leverage of both listed and unlisted companies across the globes. The literature review has tried to underscore the link between theories postulates and company leverage. However, the studies concentrated on listed companies rather than the unlisted companies in the developed world and not in the underdeveloped countries such as Tanzania. The literature reviewed reveals that capital structure concept is the most applicable to all business community today whether listed or unlisted companies.

CHAPTER THREE

RESEARCH METHODOLOGY

3.1. Introduction

The study has adopted an analytical study of Tanzanian companies, both listed and unlisted companies. The primary objective of the study is to examine the extent to which capital structure determinants influence the leverage of Tanzanian Companies. The study-specific objectives of this study as outlined in chapter one was: (a) To determine the level of leverage among Tanzanian Companies (b) To establish the extent to which liquidity influences the leverage of Tanzanian Companies. (c), To establish the extent to which profitability influences the leverage of Tanzanian Companies. (d) To examine the extent to which tangibility influences the leverage of Tanzanian Companies. (e) To establish the extent to which company size influences leverage of Tanzanian Companies. Specifically, this chapter discusses the research design, conceptual framework, and operationalization of the research variable, measurement of research variables research hypotheses, hypothesis testing, research coherence and ethical considerations.

3.2 Research Design

This is an explanatory study of listed and unlisted companies in Tanzania that utilized quantitative data. Quantitative data for this study are the financial statements of the unlisted and listed companies in Tanzania during the seven years between period 2007 and 2014. These statements include the statement of financial position and comprehensive income statement for the continuous period under the study. Quantitative data is expected to provide answers on all research questions.

3.3. Conceptual Framework

The discussion of the conceptual framework of this study is based on premises that company specific factors namely liquidity, tangibility, profitability and company Size (independent variables) tend to influence company leverage (Dependent variable). At the same time the pecking order (Majluf and Myers 1984) and Static trade off theory have relationship with company specific factors. The prediction of the pecking order assumes that Pecking order and liquidity are negatively related but the static trade off theory asserts for existence of positivism correlation between liquidity and leverage (Hamid, Bashir and Mohamed 2013). Pecking order and TOT theories both of them predict asserts that profitability and leverage are positively related. As far as tangibility is concerned pecking assumptions tangibility has positive effect on leverage which confirms the assertions of positivism relationship by the trade-off theory. These two theories also predict that a positive association exists between company size and leverage. In conclusion, the researcher intends to test if any correlations exist between these two variables among Tanzanian companies.

Figure 3.1. Study Conceptual Framework

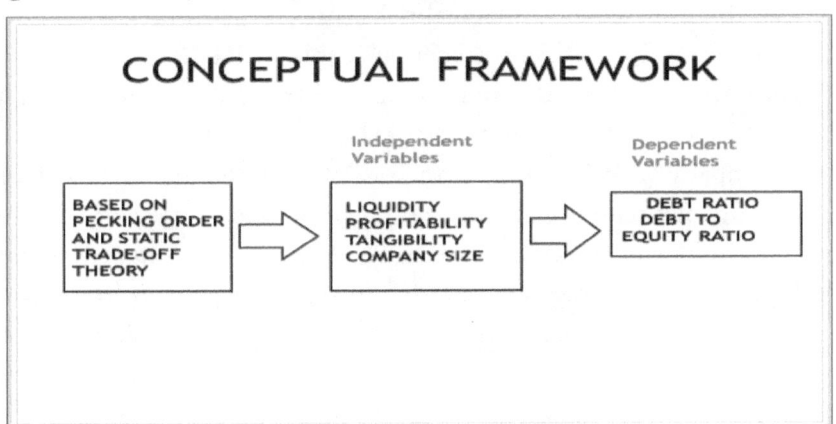

Source: Researcher Conceptualization, 2017

3.3.1 Operationalization of research variables

This study is limited to two primary study variables: The study has four independent variables namely company size, liquidity, profitability and tangibility. These variables are causative as they affect the dependent variables. (ii) Dependent variable of the study is company leverage represented by debt to equity ratio and debt ratio. They are the last group of variables in this research study. What follows in the next section is the brief discussion of these critical research Variables.

3.3.2. Independent Variables

There are many determinant factors, which are used by many previous studies as independent variables but we also select only four variables in consistency to variables used by Rajan and Zingales (1995) study which to used four independent variables to analyse capital structure across G-7 countries. This study extends the independent variable to four variables namely company size, tangibility, liquidity, and profitability.

Liquidity

We define Liquidity as the company capacity to meet its current maturing obligations by using its most liquid resources (Yona 2009). Inadequate liquidity leads to company inability to meet its current maturing obligations that lead to an increase in financial risks. According to previous studies in the literature by different academic scholar's liquidity can have an influence over the leverage as well as the performance of a company. The study by Sibilkov (2007) shows that more liquid assets increase the leverage of the company while Suhaila, Wan and Wan (2008) argued that more liquid companies tend to have less cash hence a need to use more debts A study by De Jong et al. (2008) in Croatia, Poland, and Hungary indicate that liquidity and leverage are negative correlated similar to findings by Sarja and Hale (2008) which concluded a negative relationship between liquidity and leverage.

Other studies contrary to these findings show that liquidity is positively related to the ratio of long-term debts to assets since companies with higher liquidity have easier access to debts. The positivism argument on the relationship between liquidity and leverage is also contrary to Pecking order theory. According to Pecking order theory, accumulated cash and other liquid assets create internal financing source, and therefore company would prefer using the available cash instead of debts. The study by Submitter and Anderson (2002) found that company liquidity is positively related to liquidity. Another study by Sibilkov (2009) investigated the relationship between liquidity and company leverage of public listed companies in the US and found that leverage was positively associated with liquid assets. Ankilo (2011) investigated the capital structure determinants of 66 companies in Nigeria. The results indicated that liquidity was positively related to liquidity. Sarlija and Harsh (2012) study in Croatia suggest that liquidity ratios and leverage were positively correlated. In conclusion, the study expects to test if there is a significant negative relationship between liquidity and leverage of Tanzanian companies.

Profitability

We define profitability is the company capability to generate returns from its invested assets or invested equity. It measures how the company was able to generate revenue by using the investment in assets or its equity (Yona 2008). Profitability of the company influences the level of retained earnings, which support pecking order theory of hierarchy financing. Myer's (1984) argues that adopting pecking order assumption by the profitable companies would lead them to seek funding from internal sources rather than external sources. Past profitability of a company, which at the end determines the level of retained earnings of the company, is a significant factor for companies' current capital structure.

Findings by Booth et al. (2001) reveal that profitability and leverage are negatively related showing that profitable companies have less chances of using debts but use internal sources (Retained earnings) to fund their business activities. Profitable companies usually have fewer debts since it is more accessible and cost-efficient to finance their activities by using retention money. Titman and Wessels (1988) argues that all things being equal, they would not use more debts since they can generate enough funds from internal sources.

Murinde (2004) is also supportive of retained earnings as a principal source of finance as it is considered as a cheap source of finance while Susan & Nico (2006) study on financing structure of non-listed companies in Norway suggest for positive relationship between profitability and debts. These findings are similar to a study by Long & Maltiz (1985) that found a positive relationship between profitability and leverage which supports the arguments of the trade-off theory. Further findings by Ali (2011) found that profitability has a positive influence on financial leverage. This is because chances of experiencing bankruptcy for profitable companies are minimal and such companies can access more debts at lower interest rates as compared to unprofitable companies.

Studies by Esperance et al. (2003), Hall et al. (2004) and Rajan (2005) found an adverse effect of profitability on leverage, both long-term, and short-term debt. (how comparable are these studies?)

Apart from those studies that show positive relationship between firm's characteristics and leverage several studies reveal negative relationships. Antoniou et al. (2008) study found that profitability is inversely related to leverage because of a firm's preference to raise capital from internal sources. Gill et al. (2009) study on profitability as a determinant of leverage sampled 100 companies in the USA and found that profitability and leverage are negatively related which means that there was no direct relationship between the higher profits of companies and their leverage status. This study expects to investigate if profitability of Tanzanian companies is negative related to leverage.

Tangibility

Capital structure studies reveal different types of relationship that exist between asset tangibility and leverage. Elli and Farouk (2011) and Hall (2012) recalls tangibility as the most frequently cited factors in influencing company leverage) and a major player in influencing firms leverage.

Ooi (1999) defines tangibility as the total assets held by the company. Tangibility of assets or collateral value of assets owned by a company has been found to be a determinant of leverage a (Ooi 1999). Majluf (1984) argues about asset structure as a determinant factor for capital structure choices. Companies with more assets are the ones which they can use as collateral are expected to use more debts than those with fewer assets. Shah & Thankor (1987), in their study on property companies, argue that most property development projects are financed through high leverage as equity financing becomes difficulty when projects are new. Rajan & Zing ales (1996) argues that companies with a high collateral value of assets can often borrow on relatively more favourable terms as compared to companies with high intangible assets or assets without collateral value. These findings would suggest for definite positive relationship between gearing and collateral value of assets.

Ooi (1999) study on property companies revealed that asset structure is an essential determinant of the capital structure. Booth et al. (2001), (2005) and Rajan and Zingales (2005) studies found that the asset tangibility and leverage are positively correlated in agreement to both trade off theory and pecking order theory. A study by Chen (2004) noted that. Company size is negatively related to financial structure this means that when companies become productive they increase their profitability and prefer using more of retained earnings to fund their operations. The findings are not in contradiction to the assumptions of the pecking order.

Fitmi & Deari (2009) studied the capital structure of Macedonian companies both listed and unlisted ones for years between 2005 and 2009. The study findings suggest that tangibility and leverage is negatively correlated. The findings confirmed the pecking order assumptions that tangibility negatively influences company leverage. The reasons for this are that companies with lower levels of tangible assets are more subject to information asymmetry problems, and therefore preferring to finance their business operations with debts. Morri (2009) study suggests that company asset size can directly influence the amounts of debts that the company can use. However, the validity of the above arguments is not the same in the service industry. Gill et al. (2009) study on Services sector in the USA revealed that leverage decreases as the proportion to the increase in total company assets normally the fixed assets just because the service industry is usually characterized by a relatively low level of fixed assets.

Bundala and Machogu (2012) found that tangibility was a second significant capital structure determinant in Tanzania listed companies and was negatively correlated with and asset tangibility was negatively related to the financial leverage which means that companies with more fixed assets employ fewer debts in financing their business operations.

According to Pecking order theory, tangible assets affects the leverage of companies and it is assumed that tangibility is positively related to company leverage. Confirmation of this prediction is evidenced by other different studies. Booth et al. (2001), Gaud et al. (2005) and Rajan and Zingales studies found that asset structure of a company is positively related to a capital structure of the firm which was consistent with both pecking order and trade-off theory. Frank and Goyal (2003) study found that as tangible assets level increases companies' level of leverage also increases since companies tend to use the assets as their collateral for debt hence that their high share increases the leverage. These findings are further supported by other scholars. Akhtar (2005) studied the Australian companies and found that collateral assets were the important determinant of debt ratio.

Myer and Majluf (1984) laid down the assumptions of the trade -off theory that company net fixed assets are positive correlated to leverage as companies' tendency of using collateral leads them to have easy access to external funds. This prediction is confirmed by Frank and Goyal (2006) study which reveal that asset tangibility is positively related to company leverage. These studies confirmed the prediction of the trade-off theory.

However, other studies negate both the prediction of the pecking order theory and Trade-off Theory on the relationship between tangibility and leverage by showing a negative relationship between these variables. More assets reduce the information asymmetry level hence leading to cheaper equity (Harris and Ravis 1991). According to Cornell et al. (1996), study findings revealed a negative relationship exists between tangibility and leverage ratio.

Pandey (2001) also found that there was a significant negative correlation between tangibility and debt ratios similar to the previous findings by De Angelo and Masulis (1980) study. A study by Chen (2004) noted a negative relationship between company assets and financial structure which was in line with pecking order theory on the emphasis that when companies become more significant, they tend to have enough profits and therefore prefer to use more of their retained earnings to finance their assets. Fitmi & Deari (2009) study on determinants of capital structure of Macedonian listed and unlisted companies for period 2005-2009 found that tangibility is negatively associated with leverage and is consistent with the implication of pecking order theory for both listed and listed companies which is similar to Gaud et al. (2005) findings. The reasons for this are because companies with lower levels of tangible assets are more subject to information asymmetry problems, and therefore willing to use debts to finance their activities.

Morri (2009) study suggests that company asset size can directly influence some debts that the company can use. However, the validity of the above arguments is not the same in the service industry. Gill et al. (2009) study on Services sector in the USA revealed that leverage decreases as the proportion of fixed assets in the total assets of the firm increases just because the service industry is usually characterized by a relatively low level of fixed assets. Bundala and Machogu (2012) study of listed companies in Tanzania found that tangibility was a second significant capital structure determinant for listed companies and was negatively correlated with the financial leverage which means that companies with high level of fixed assets employ fewer debts in their capital structure. In this study, we expect to find out if their positive relationship between assets tangibility and company leverage.

Company size

Titman and Wessels (1988) considers company size as the logarithm of net sales. Padron et al. (2005) used the logarithm of total assets to measure company size. This study will adopt logarithm of Net sales to measure company size as this has been a standard measure of company size by other previous studies. Company size also determines the capital structure (Scott: 1977). His argument is more on the size of the company as a determinant factor for debt-equity choice. According to Smith (1977), large companies are likely to be highly indebted since the cost of equity issue is higher. Small companies are more dependent on short-term loans rather than on long terms while large companies will use equity and long terms debts. This characterizes Tanzanian companies as far as debt access is concerned. Small companies in Tanzanian have no adequate collaterals and high interest rates given by lending institutions impairs these companies to raise funds through long-term debts.

Castanias (1983) argues that more major companies will have higher debts as lenders will be willing to provide debts. Kim and Sorenson (1986) support the argument by adding that larger firms are less risky to grant debts. An empirical study by Titman and Wessels (1988) suggest for negative correlation between size and leverage while Harris and Ravin (1991) study which suggest that firm size is positively related to leverage. This study predicts similar findings in Tanzania. Arêtye (1994) study in Ghana found that small companies have a more significant problem with credit than larger company's do which concurs with Rajan and Zingales (1995) who concluded that firm size and leverage are positively related. Oio (1999) argues about the size of companies and its influence on accessibility to equity financing. His study reveals that small companies do not have much choice between equity and debts but have to rely on bank loans. Booth et al. (2001) confirmed firms' size and leverage of companies are positively related while Panno (2003) argues about the importance of positive relationship between size and leverage. Akhtar and Oliver (2009) and Ali (2011) studies found that firm size was significant and positively related to financial leverage. Studies by Ghazonami (2013) and Wahapand and Ramli (2014) indicate a significant negative relationship between company size and debt ratio.

Further discussion on the link between trade off theory prediction and leverage reveal different types of association between the two variables. Songul (2014) argued that the trade-off theory predict that large companies are characterized by the tendency of being more diversified, less risk and less prone to bankruptcy. Therefore, such companies may prefer to use more debts rather than equity in financing their activities as opposed to small companies. The findings by Bundala and Machogu (2011) in their study of capital structure determinants of non-financial listed companies in Tanzania indicate that company size is positively related to financial leverage. This study is expected to test if there is company size is negatively related to leverage of Tanzanian companies.

Measurement for Independent Variables

Liquidity

According to Ghasema and Ab Razak (2016), liquidity is the key indicator that measures whether the company can fulfil its debts commitment by using its liquid assets. There are different measures of the liquidity namely current ratio (CR) and the Quick ratio (QR). In this study, Liquidity is measured by using current ratio. This is the measure of the extent to which the company can meet its current maturing obligation by using its liquid resources.

$$\text{CURRENT RATIO} = \frac{\text{CURRENT ASSETS}}{\text{CURRENT LIABILITIES}}$$

Profitability

Different scholars in different studies have used different measures to measure profitability. Measures of profitability include the Return on Assets (ROA) and Return on Equity (ROE). In their studies, Titman & Wessels (1988) used operating income divided by total assets while Rajan & Zingales (1995) study and OzKan (2001) used return on assets as a measure of profitability. Another scholar who used the same measurement was Wafaa (2010) while Jose Lopez (2003) used earnings before interest and taxes divided by total assets. In this study, we adopt both returns on Assets (ROA) and Return on equity (ROE) as a measure of profitability. The challenges of using accounting ratio are that there are many ratios one can decide to use to measure company profitability without being restricted by any standard as the international financial reporting standard do not provide any specific formula to measure profitability.

PROFITABILITY = RETURN ON ASSETS (1)

PROFITABILITY = RETURN ON EQUITY (2).

Tangibility

Tangibility represents the total assets of the firm. Different measures are used to measure tangibility. LaRocca et al (2009) did use the ratio of between total property and Equipment and total book assets to measure tangibility. In this study the ratio of fixed assets to total assets is used to measure tangibility which is consistent to measurement used by Rajan and Zingales (1995) and Wessels (1998). Other scholars who used the same ratio to measure tangibility include Koksal (2013), Psilluke and Daskalakis (2008). This study also adopts tangibility as the ratio of fixed assets to total assets.

$$\text{TANGIBILITY} = \frac{\text{FIXED ASSETS}}{\text{TOTAL ASSETS}}$$

Company Size

Titman & Wessels (1988) study used the logarithm of net sales as a measure of company size, and Drobetz and Fix (2003) measured company size as the natural logarithm of net sales. They argued that net sales be a better proxy for sales because many companies tend to keep their reported size as small as possible (explain). Other previous studies also confirm the use of natural logarithm of sales as the measure of company size (Myers and Majluf 1984, Titman and Wessels, 1988. Padron et al. 2005 and Turere 2012). This study will also adopt the same measure of the logarithm of Net sales to measure company size.

COMPANY SIZE = LOGARITHM OF SALES

The table below summarizes the proxy measurement that of the independent variables of the study

Table 3.1 Proxy Measurement of Independent Variables

Variable	Measurement	Comparable Study
Size	logarithm of net sales	Padron et al (2005)
Liquidity	Current RATIO = $\frac{Current\ Assets}{Current\ Liabilities}$	Submitter and Anderson (2002) Ankilo (2011), Ahmed and Arris (2015)
Profitability	Return on Assets (ROA) = $\frac{Profit\ After\ tax}{Total\ Assets}$ Return on Equity (ROA) = $\frac{Profit\ After\ tax}{Total\ Equity}$	Titman & Wessels (1988) Rajan & Zingales (1995) OzKan (2001), Wafaa (2010), Jose Lopez-Gracia (2003)
Tangibility	$\frac{Fixed\ Assets}{Total\ Assets}$	Koksal 2013, Psillake and Daskalakis (2008) and Rajan & Zingales (1995)

Source: Researcher 2017

3.3.3 Dependent Variables

Dependent variables are the outcomes mostly affected by the independent variables. The study adopts leverage as a dependent variable. Voulgaris et al. (2004) define leverage as the amount of foreign capital (liabilities) as shown on the balance sheet. Correia et al. (2006) define leverage as the relative use of debt in the capital structure. Scholars from different parts of the world use different types of indicators to measure leverage. In the study by Hall et al. (2006) debt to total assets was used to measure leverage (book value). Rajan and Zingales (1995) propounded the use of both long-term debt ratios and short-term debt ratios. In this study we use two measures of leverage namely debt to equity ratio and debt ratio:

Measuring Leverage

In this study, we used book value debt to equity ratio and debt ratio as measures of leverage for both unlisted and listed companies in Tanzania.

We define leverage as Debt to equity ratio which is total liabilities divided by equity plus total debt and Debt ratio as total debt divided by total equity. This measurement is consistent with other studies on capital structure.

Table 3.2. Proxy Measurement for Dependent Variable

Variable	Measurement	Comparable Study
Debt to Equity Ratio	$\dfrac{\text{Total Debts}}{\text{Total Equity + Total Debts}}$	Hall et al. (2006)
Debt Ratio	$\dfrac{\text{Total Debts}}{\text{Total Equity}}$	Correia et al. (2006)

Source: Researcher 2017

3.4. Research Hypotheses

The hypotheses formulation of this study is by the reviewed current capital structure determinants literature and research objectives of the study under section 1.6 above. Five main research hypotheses are formulated to understand the correlation between capital structure determinants namely company liquidity, profitability, tangibility, size and leverage among Tanzanian Companies. The following primary hypotheses are formulated together with their minor hypotheses.

Hypothesis 1

Hypothesis, one is formulated with objective of understanding the degree of leverage between unlisted and listed companies. Literature reveal that that listed companies tend to be large in size as compared to unlisted companies with more collateral hence be able to have access to bank loans while small companies which majority of them they don't have such access.

H1: There is a significance difference in leverage between listed and unlisted companies in Tanzania

This hypothesis s was tested with other two minor hypotheses

H1: 1a: There is a significance difference in debt to equity ratio between listed and unlisted companies in Tanzania
H1: 1b: There is a significance difference in debt ratio between listed and unlisted companies in Tanzania

Hypothesis two (H2) is formulated with the aim of understanding the relationship between liquidity and company leverage. The basis of the hypothesis also considers the capital structure theories (pecking order theory, the static trade-off) postulates on company leverage Pecking order predicts a negative relationship between liquidity and company leverage while the Trade-off theory assumes that liquidity and leverage are positively related. Management of liquidity is an essential factor for a timely meeting of company financial and operating expenses without causing unnecessary financial distress. Submitter and Anderson (2002) study found a positive relationship between liquid assets and company debts. In context of Nigerian companies, Ankilo (2011) studied the relationship between leverage and liquidity. Study findings indicate that liquidity had significant positive impact on leverage. These findings were consistent with the trade-off theory. However, other studies have revealed a negative relationship between liquidity and leverage (Mahmoud and Zakaria 2007, Ahmad and Arris 2015). On the basis of these arguments; Hypothesis two is formulated hereunder:

H2: There is a significant negative relationship between liquidity and leverage of Tanzanian companies

Hypothesis one has another two minor hypotheses stated hereunder

H2: 2a: There is a significant negative relationship between liquidity and debt to equity ratio.
H2: 2b: There is a significant negative relationship between liquidity and debt ratio.

The formulation of hypothesis three (H3) is on the basis of empirical literature and assumptions of the pecking order theory to confirm that profitability and company leverage are related. Different studies have revealed the different relationship between profitability and company leverage. Hall et al. (2000) study found profitability was not statistically significant to leverage though Long and Maltzi (1986) suggest that profitability and leverage are not related. According to Booth et al. (2001) and Antoniou et al. (2007) profitability and leverage were negatively correlated but consistent to the Pecking order assumptions that companies with higher profits would prefer using internal sources (Retained earnings) instead of borrowing. Ahmed (2007) also found that profitability and company leverage were not correlated. By pecking order assumptions and evidenced empirical literature the following hypothesis is formulated

H3: There is a significant negative relationship between company profitability and leverage of Tanzanian Companies

Hypothesis three has another two minor hypotheses stated hereunder

H3: 3a: There is a significant negative relationship between ROE and leverage of Tanzanian Companies
H3: 3b: There is a significant negative relationship between ROA and leverage of Tanzanian Companies

Hypothesis four (H4) aims at testing the relationship between tangibility and leverage following the predictions of the two prominent capital structures namely trade off theory and pecking order theory. Um (2001) studied Korean companies and found that tangibility and leverage are positive correlated similar to the findings of Dan (2002) which indicated that tangibility has positive significant impact on company leverage. Olahula and Oni (2014) assessed the impact of tangibility on leverage among listed companies in Nigeria and found that there was a definite non-significant correlation between tangibility and leverage. The same positive relationship between asset tangibility and leverage are also revealed by other studies (Mayers 1990: Rajan and Zingales 1995). There are other study findings that reveal a negative relationship between tangibility and leverage such as the ones by Booth et al. (2001) while supporting the pecking order theory and trade off theory. Rajan and Zingales (1995) findings also reveal that tangibility has significant negative impact on leverage in support of the e pecking order.

Harc (2014) study on Croatian SME's on the relationship between tangibility and capital structure show that asset tangibility and short -term leverage are negatively correlated assets and short-term leverage (Supporting the pecking order theory) but tangibility and long- term leverage is positively correlated which supports the trade-off theory. Based on these argument discussions and assumptions of the pecking order and trade-off theory we formulate the following hypothesis

H4: There is a positive relationship between assets tangibility and company leverage.

Hypothesis five has another two minor hypotheses stated hereunder

H4: 4a: There is a positive relationship between assets tangibility and debt to equity ratio
H4: 4b: There is a positive relationship between assets tangibility and debt ratio

Hypothesis five (H5) is formulated on the assumptions of the trade-off theory and the literature to understand the relationship between company leverage and company size. The review of the various empirical studies shows different types of relationship that exist between company size and leverage. Modigliani and Miller (1958) assumed a no relationship between company size and leverage. However, different scholars who further studied the relationship between company size and leverage found different relationships. Titman (1988) supports the positive relationship between leverage and company Size. According to Chuen and Song (2002) size and leverage have significant positive relationship. found a significant relationship between leverage and company size. In their study in Hungary, Bela and Mateus (2002) study reveal that size and leverage are positively related. Their findings were inharmony with the trade-off theory. In another study, Cassar and Holmes (2003) found the existence of a positive relationship between company size and leverage among larger companies. The reasons for larger companies having high level of leverage is because of having lower default rates as compared to small companies. A similar study by Elliot (2007) of 129 Greece companies showed a positive relationship between size and company leverage. Also, findings by Sbeit (2010) found a same positive correlation between size and leverage which is in consistent to the predictions of the trade -off theory. Based on these findings and assumptions of the trade-off theory we, therefore, formulate the following hypothesis

H5: There is a significant negative relationship between company size and leverage of Tanzanian Companies

Hypothesis two has another two minor hypotheses stated hereunder

H5: 5a: There is a significant negative relationship between company size and debt to equity ratio
H5: 5b: There is a significant negative relationship between company size and debt ratio

3.5. Hypothesis Testing

Vincent (2006) explains that hypothesis testing is the rational framework for applying statistical tests. A statistical test is an inferential process based on probability, which you can use to conclude the population parameters. Hypothesis testing follows the following three logic steps; A hypothesis concerning a population is stated, select a sample from the population and use of sample data to determine whether it is reasonably to support or not to support the hypothesis. Ultimately, the conclusion drawn is about the population, not just the sample. There are various methods of testing research hypothesis.

This study used a t-test, correlation test and regression analysis to test if there is any association between capital structure determinant factors (independent variables) and leverage (Dependent variable). The research adopted the various statistical test to test the Null hypothesis. To understand the association and the strength of capital structure determinant factors and leverage the study used correlation and regression analysis. Pearson Correlation tests measures the strength of the relationship regression variables under study.

Table 3.3. Hypothesis Techniques

Hypotheses	Statistical Testing Technique
H1: There is a significance difference in leverage between listed and unlisted companies in Tanzania	Pearson Correlation and Regression Analysis
H2: There is a significant negative relationship between Liquidity and leverage of Tanzanian companies	Pearson Correlation and Regression Analysis
H3: There is a significant negative relationship between company profitability and leverage of Tanzanian Companies	Pearson Correlation and Regression Analysis
H4: There is a positive relationship between assets tangibility and company leverage	Pearson Correlation and Regression Analysis
H5; There is a significant negative relationship between company size and leverage of Tanzanian Companies	Pearson Correlation and Regression Analysis

Source: Researcher 2017

3.6. Research Coherence

Best Practices for research work require the harmony of research objectives with the research objectives, research hypothesis, and the study variables. The following table (Table 3.4) summarizes the research objectives and shows their coherence with research questions and research hypotheses as well as the independent and dependent variable of the study. Research coherence creates reliability of the study.

Table 3.4 Research Coherence

Research Objectives	Research Question	Hypotheses	Variables
(1) To establish the degree of leverage among listed and unlisted companies in Tanzania	What is the significance difference on leverage of among Tanzanian companies?	H1: There is a significance difference in leverage between listed and unlisted companies in Tanzania	Independent Company Type Dependent Variable - Leverage

2. To examine the extent to which liquidity influences the leverage of Tanzanian Companies	To what extent liquidity influences the leverage of Tanzanian companies?	H2: There is a significant negative relationship between Liquidity and leverage of Tanzanian companies	Independent Liquidity Dependent Leverage
3. To examine the extent to which profitability influences the leverage of Tanzanian Companies	To what extent profitability influences the leverage of Tanzanian companies?	H3: Profitability and leverage of Tanzanian companies are negatively correlated	Independent Profitability Dependent Leverage
4. To examine the extent to which tangibility influences the leverage of Tanzanian Companies	To what extent tangibility influences the leverage of Tanzanian companies?	H4: There is a positive relationship between assets tangibility and company leverage	Independent Tangibility Dependent Leverage
5. To establish the extent to which company size influences leverage of Tanzanian Companies.	To what extent does company size influence the leverage of Tanzanian companies?	H5: There is a significant negative relationship between company size and leverage of Tanzanian Companies	Independent Size Dependent Leverage

Source: Researcher 2017

3.7. Model Development

Given the subject of this research, the conceptual framework is focused on testing the multiple models. The assumed association between company liquidity, profitability, tangibility company size and capital leverage. To understand the correlation or the association of the study explanatory variables, linear regression models are used to estimate the relationship between independent variables and leverage and capital structure (namely Liquidity, Profitability and Tangibility, size) and company leverage.

To test the relationship between liquidity (Current ratio) and company leverage two models (Model 1 and Model 2) were used. The models used liquidity as an independent variable and the dependent variable is leverage. Company leverage is measured by Debt ratio and Debt to Equity Ratio. The models are presented hereunder;

DEBT RATIO i, t = ß0+ ß1 (CR i, t) + e   Model (1)
DEBT TO EQUITY i, t = ß0+ ß1 (CR i, t) +e   Model (2)

    Where:
        ß1 (C Ratio i, t) = The Current Ratio of company i at time t
        ß2 (Quick Ratio i, t) = The Quick Ratio of company i at time t
        ß0= Constant variable
        ß1= Coefficients of regression
        e = Standard error

The testing of relationship between profitability and leverage used two models (Model 3 and Model 4). All models use profitability as an independent variable and company leverage as a dependent variable. (Debt ratio, Debt to Equity Ratio) The models are presented hereunder:

DEBT RATIO i, t = ß0+ ß1 (ROA i, t) + ß2 (ROE i, t) + e   Model (3)
DEBT TO EQUITY RATIO i, t = ß0+ ß1 (ROA i, t) + ß2(ROE i, t) + e   Model (4)

Where:

ß1 (ROA i, t) The Return on Assets of company i at time t
ß2(ROE i, t) The Return on Equity of company i at time t
ß0= Constant variable
ß1= Coefficients of regression
e = Standard error

Finally, simple regression model 5 and Model 6 tests the relationship between the relationship between companies' tangibility (independent variable) and company leverage (Debt ratio, Debt to Equity Ratio). The models are hereunder:

DEBT RATIO i, t = ß0+ ß1 (TANG i, t) + e　　　　　　　Model (5)
DEBT TO EQUITY RATIO i, t = ß0+ ß1 (TANG i, t) + e　　Model (6)

Where:

ß1 (TANG i, t) Tangibility of company i at time t
ß0= Constant variable
ß1= Coefficients of regression
e = Standard error

Furthermore, Model 7 and Model 8 were applied to test the relationship company size (independent variable) and leverage (Dependent Variable). The following model depicted below indicates the regression between size and leverage

DEBT RATIO i, t = ß0+ ß1 (SIZE i, t) + e　　　　　　　Model (7)
DEBT TO EQUITY RATIO i, t = ß0+ ß1 (SIZE i, t) + e　　Model (8)

Where:

ß1 (SIZE i, t) The Size of company i at time t
ß0= Constant variable
ß1= Coefficients of regression
e = Standard error

3.8. Study Area

The study area was in Dar-es-salaam, Arusha, Moshi and Mwanza Tanzania. These are the prominent regions in Tanzania hosting a majority of headquarters of majority companies. At the same time, these were selected because these are leading commercial cities in the country considered having more economic activities and therefore they were likely to have more companies than other regions.

3.9. Study Population

The population of this study will comprise of all listed and unlisted businesses that are a member of the Confederation of Industries in Tanzania (CTI) which were members by the end of the year 2014. Tanzania had a total number of 280 companies registered by CTI by the end of the year 2014

3.10. Sample Size and Sampling Technique

In selecting the sample size for this study, stratified sampling method was used to pick the representative unlisted and listed companies in various sectors of the economy to provide answers to the research questions. Study sample is picked from unquoted businesses that reported financial statements every year during the year 2007-2014 selected from members of CTI (Confederation of Tanzanian Industries) database as well as 19 listed companies in Dar-es-salaam Stock Exchange. The database contained information of 280 businesses that were registered by the end of the year 2014.

The companies selected for study were according to specific inclusion criteria's. The sample excludes all banks and other financial institutions, utility and telecommunication companies as well as all other services provision companies. The other inclusion criterion is that selected company's fiscal year should be ending on 31st Dec or 30 June of each year. Based on the inclusion criteria above forty-six (46) unlisted companies and thirteen listed companies (13) were chosen as a representative sample. These companies were selected from the different economic sector. Table 3.4 below gives the summary of all companies taken as a representative sample of the study

Table 3.5- Sampling Frame- Selected Companies

Sector	Unlisted	Listed	Total
Agriculture	2	0	2
Air Transport	0	1	1
Automobile	1	0	1
Aviation	1	0	1
Energy	3	0	3

Beverage	4	2	6
Food Processing	0	1	1
IT Companies	1	0	1
Construction	9	0	9
Telecommunication	2	1	3
Hospitality (Hotels)	6	0	6
Tourism	3	0	3
Printing and Publication	2	0	2
Manufacturing	3	4	7
Media Companies	2	1	3
Real Estate	2	0	2
Wholesale Company	2	0	2
Mining	3	3	6
Total	46	13	59

Source: Researcher 2017

3.11. Data Collection Method

The study collected Panel data from financial statements of 59 companies from different economic sectors for seven years beginning the year 2007 to 2014 to provide answers to all five research questions. Financial statements information was used to calculate various financial ratios that are useful in measuring capital structure determinant factors as well as company leverage (dependent variable). We assume the sample of Panel data to be substantial over the period of study, and this confirms to the justification of this collection method. The application of panel data is relevant where the sample size is large.

3.12. Data Analysis

Analysing data for this study involved the use of excel spreadsheet and Statistical Package (SPSS). We tabulated the financial statements information in excel spread sheet, coded them and there after the data was captured into a statistical package. After that, analysed the data to obtain the descriptive statistics, trend analysis, t-test analysis, correlation analysis as well as the regression analysis to test the study hypotheses and ensuring the achievement of the research objectives.

To analyse the data related to company liquidity and leverage, we examined the aggregate trend analysis of liquidity (Current Ratio) for both listed and unlisted companies. The use of t-test statistics was important to identify significant differences in liquidity among listed and unlisted companies. Furthermore, Pearson correlation and simple regression model analysis specified hereunder was applied to understand the relationship between company's liquidity (Independent variable) and leverage (Dependent Variable).

To analyse the data related to company profitability and leverage, we examined the aggregate trend analysis of profitability (ROA and ROE) for both listed and unlisted companies. The use of t-test statistics was essential to identify significant differences in profitability among companies. Furthermore, simple regression analysis is applied to understand the relationship between profitability (independent variable) and leverage (Debt ratio, Debt to Equity Ratio) as the dependent variable.

The analysis of data related to company tangibility and leverage involved the use of aggregate trend analysis of tangibility (Total ASSETS) for both listed and unlisted companies. The use of t-test statistics was used to identify significant differences in fixed assets tangibility among companies. Furthermore, simple regression analysis is applied to understand the relationship between Tangibility (independent variable) and leverage (Debt ratio, Debt to Equity Ratio).

To analyse the data related to company size and leverage, we examined the descriptive statistics (Mean score, Standard Deviation, minimum, maximum,) of company's net sales, trend analysis of net sales (log of sales) for both listed and unlisted companies. The use of t-test statistics was essential to identify significant differences in size among companies. Furthermore, correlation and Pearson regression analysis are applied to understand the relationship between company size (independent variable) and leverage (Dependent Variable).

3.13. Multicorreleranity Tests

The study adopted the Variance Inflation Factor (VIF) to check any multicolliearnity problem between independent and dependent variables in regression models. The Variance inflation factor for all regressions models (Model 1 to Model 8) indicated a test VIF test below 10 which means that there was no any Multicorreleranity problem between the regression variables.

3.14 Ethical Consideration

The study gathered information from the financial statements of both listed and unlisted companies. It was easy to gather the information from the listed companies as most of the financial statements are published and available from public web domain of these companies. Because of confidential nature of unlisted companies and difficulty of obtaining the financial statements only few companies financial managers were willing to provide the audited financial statements hence limiting the number of unlisted company's participation in the study.

3.15 Summary and Conclusion.

This chapter describes the methodological process of the entire study. The chapter has clearly elaborated the research design and the conceptual framework of the study and explains in details the operationalization of the research variables. It further explains how the independent and dependent variables were measured. The chapter has also explained the methods used to test all the research hypotheses of this study. It further shows the coherence of both variables of the study with the research objectives and research questions. The chapter further explained the study area, study population, sampling frame and sample size of companies involved in the study. At the end of the chapter ethical consideration of the study are highlighted ending with the summary and conclusions

CHAPTER FOUR

RESEARCH FINDINGS

4.1 Introduction

The chapter provides information on summary statistics and detailed findings of each research question, hypothesis testing and discussions of the research findings for each research questions. The chapter also provides the conclusions made on the study as well give policy recommendations for practitioners, academicians as well as give recommendations for further research. The presentations of the findings are presented hereunder:

4.2. Summary Statistics

This section summarizes the study findings of the companies chosen for the study and it includes the findings on companies listed on Dar-es-salaam stock exchange (DSE) and unlisted companies already registered by the Business Registration Board of Tanzania (BRELA) by the end of the year 2014. Following the exclusion criteria adopted by this study, data collection excludes all service organizations and financial services institution such as the insurance companies and the commercial banks.

Listed Companies

The study used panel data of 13 listed companies in Dar-es-salaam Stock Exchange (DSE)by the end of the year 2014 (Annex1) drawn from the financial statements for years 2007 throughout to year 2014. These companies include Tanzania Oxygen Limited, Tanzania Breweries Companies, Tatepa Company Limited, Tanga Cement, Swissport Tanzania Limited, Tanzania Portland Cement Public Limited, Precision Air, Swala Gas and Oil Ltd., Kenya Airways, East African Breweries, Nation Media Group, Acacia Mining and Tanzania Cigarette Company.

Unlisted Companies

Based on exclusion criteria, a total of 46 selected unlisted companies were selected from different economic sectors (Annex 2). The selected companies included companies from beverage sector, construction industry, hospitality, mining, power generation, textiles, and Transportation sector. We also exclude all unlisted financial institutions because of different characteristics of their financial statements.

4.3. Findings: Degree of Leverage of Unlisted and Listed Companies in Tanzania

4.3.1 Introduction

This section presents the summary statistics on statements of financial positions, findings on the overall degree of leverage of the selected Tanzanian companies and the trend analysis of both debt ratios and debt ratios as well as the company financial position among the listed and unlisted companies of Tanzania, hypothesis testing and discussions on the research findings in consistency with previous studies and study theories, conclusions and recommendations. We re-state research question one (RQ1) here under *"What is the degree of leverage among Tanzanian unlisted and listed companies?"* The presentations of the results are presented hereunder:

4.3.2 Summary Statistics

We give below the summary statistics of financial positions of the 59 companies both listed and unlisted companies for the period of 8 years beginning the year 2007 to the year 2014. The summary statistics is the discussed below

Financial Positions

Table 4.1 shows the descriptive statistics of the representative samples from both companies (Listed and unquoted companies) in Tanzania. The table gives the summary statistics of companies' assets over the selected period. As far as current assets are concerned, listed companies show a mean value of current assets for 53 observations was Tshs 62,929m with standard deviation of Tshs 82,387m and minimum and higher values of Tshs 194.1m and Tshs 353,420 respectively. At the same time, results for unlisted companies show mean (SD)value of current assets for 213 observations Tshs 51,836m with standard deviation of Tshs 160,955m and minimum and maximum value of Tshs 1.473m and Tshs 1,490m respectively. These results reveal a significant difference among these companies, listed companies having more current assets as compared to the ones not listed. The lowest listed company having a minimum of Tshs 194.1m in current assets and highest company having Tshs 353,420m in current assets over this period of research as compared to a minimum of Tshs 1.49 m in current assets and a maximum of Tshs 1473m for the unlisted companies. These findings also indicate that unlisted companies have challenges of working capital as compared to listed companies.

As far as fixed assets are concerned, the results show the mean value of fixed assets for 53 observations for unquoted companies was Tshs 104,728m with standard deviation of Tshs 132,962m with minimum and maximum value of Tshs 223,507 and Tshs 526,194 respectively. However, results for unlisted companies for 213 observations show a mean value of fixed assets of Tshs 70,305m with standard deviation of Tshs 184,052m with minimum and maximum value of Nil and TSHS 1,492m respectively. These findings suggest that listed companies have more fixed assets than the unlisted companies.

Finally, the results for total assets in 53 observations of listed companies show a mean value of 104,426m with standard deviation of Tshs 133.1m with minimum and maximum value of Tshs 526.1m and Tshs 14,615m respectively. The total assets for unlisted companies in 213 observations show a mean (SD) value of Tshs 64,001m [Tshs 156,660m] with minimum and maximum value of Tshs 0 and Tshs 1064.26m respectively. This also shows that companies not listed have less assets than the listed companies.

Table 4.1 Summary Company Financial position (Assets) in Million Tshs

Construct	Variable	**Listed**	**Unlisted**
Current Assets	Mean	62.929	51,836
	Standard Deviation	82,387	160,955
	Min	194,178	1473,796
	Maximum	353,420	1,490,718
	Observation	53	213
Fixed Assets	Mean	104,787	70305
	Standard Deviation	132,962	184052
	Min	223,507	0
	Maximum	526,194	1,492,189
	Observation	53	213
Total Assets	Mean	104,426	64001
	Standard Deviation	133,185	156660
	Min	526, 194	0
	Maximum	14,615,630	1, 064,262
	Observation	53	213

Source: Researcher 2017

As far as companies' financial position in terms of equity and liabilities, the table below (Table 5.2) shows the state of differences between two categories of companies namely the unlisted and the listed companies. On equity, the listed companies have higher mean scores (SD) of Tshs 192.2m with standard deviation of Tsh155.9m in 53 observations as compared to unlisted companies with mean value of Tshs 156.44M and standard deviation of Tshs 148m.The results mean that listed companies do highly finance their business activities by using equity rather than debts. Study findings reveal that the lowest listed company has a minimum equity of Tshs 6.503 billion and highest company having Tshs 451.73 billion over this period of research as compared to a minimum of Tshs172.65m and a maximum of Tshs 451 billion for the unlisted companies.

As far as long-term liabilities are concerned, listed companies have higher mean scores (SD) of Tshs 54.8m [Tshs 58.1m] against mean score (SD) of Tshs 41.9m[54.2m] of that of unlisted companies showing that listed companies have more long-term liabilities as compared to the unlisted companies. On average the minimum amount of long-term liabilities by listed companies is Tshs 636m and the maximum long-term liabilities borrowed by listed company is Tshs 153,882 m while the average minimum long-term liabilities by the unlisted companies is Tshs 160m and maximum amount is Tshs 153,882m. The results also show that listed companies have higher mean scores (SD) of Tshs 133.6m [Tshs 101.65m] against lower mean score (SD) of Tshs 100.48(Tshs 103.99m). These findings show that listed companies borrow more on short terms than the unlisted companies. On the other side, the amount borrowed by listed companies ranged from a minimum Tshs 1.579m to maximum of Tshs 2.97.849m as compared to the minimum amount of Tshs 985m to a maximum amount of Tshs 297,849m.

Table 4.2: Summary of Company Financial Positions (Equity + Liabilities)

Construct	Variable	Listed	Unlisted
Equity	Mean	100,518,384	68,408,672
	Standard Deviation	126,078,027	182,251,863
	Min	223,507,607	0
	Maximum	526,194,000	1,492,189,480
	Observation	53	213
Current Liabilities	Mean	11,836,863	17,344,904
	Standard Deviation	16,854,506	60,468,781
	Min	94,569,000	0
	Maximum	147,417,774	457,120,788

	Observation	53	208
Non–Current Liabilities	Mean	65,112,960	38,113,387
	SD	79,545,038	114,758,540
	Min	0	0
	Maximum	317,272,000	1,057,411,403
	Observation	53	213
Total Debts	Mean	25,303,760	14,710,533
	SD	40,778,195	38,064,696
	Min	62,081,411	240,106
	Maximum	180,959,000	206,116,266
	Observation	53	266

Source: Researcher Data 2017

Trend Analysis of Company Leverages

Over a period of study leverage ratio of both companies has been changing. Table 4.3 and Figure 4.1 show that debt to equity ratio of unlisted companies had a higher increase as compared to debt to equity ratio of the listed companies. In the year 2007, unlisted companies had higher mean values in debt to equity ratio of (X=0.47) against the mean value of (X=0.33) against that of the listed companies. In the year 2008 debt to equity ratio of unlisted companies did not change while there was an increase of 33% of the listed companies' debt to equity ratio. In the following year 2009, there was a decrease by 11% of debt to equity ratio of the listed companies against a decrease of 9% for the unlisted companies. In the year 2010, both companies had a slight increase of 9% (Listed companies) and 7% (listed companies) respectively. In the year 2012 listed companies' debt to equity ratio increased by 6% and unlisted companies' debt to equity ratio decreased by 4%. The following year (2013) debt to equity ratio increased only by 6% for unlisted companies and 48% for listed companies. The high growth of debt to equity ratio for listed companies shows greater variations caused by individual characteristics of the listed companies.

Table 4:3. Trend Analysis: Debt to Equity Ratio

Year	Listed Companies		Unlisted Companies	
	Mean	% change	Mean	% Change
2007	0.33		0.47	0%
2008	0.44	33%	0.47	0%
2009	0.39	-11%	0.43	-9%
2010	0.43	10%	0.46	7%
2011	0.47	9%	0.49	7%
2012	0.53	13%	0.47	-4%
2013	0.56	6%	0.54	15%
2014	0.83	48%	0.57	6%

Source: Researcher 2017

Figure 4.1 Debt to Equity Ratio of Tanzanian Companies

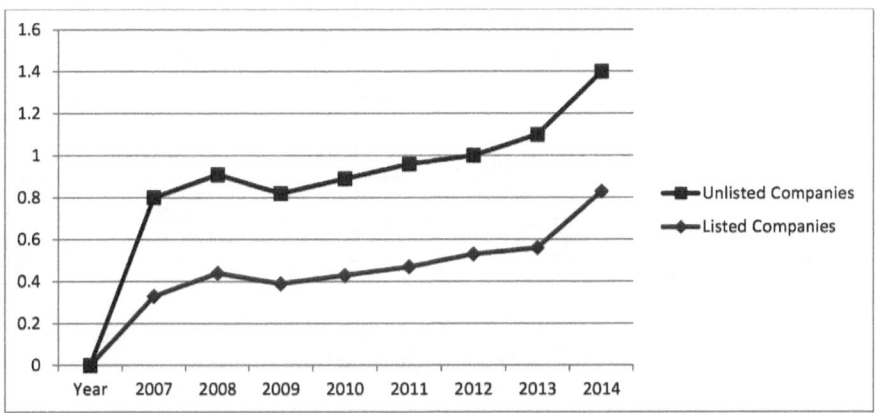

Source: Researcher 2017

Table 4.4 and figure 4.2 reveals trend data for debt ratio. These data show a trend of mixed direction over the year of study (2007-2014). In 2007 unlisted companies had higher mean values in debt ratio of 1.89 as compared to 0.55 of that of listed companies. In 2008 the debt ratio of listed companies increased by 45% as compared to decrease of unlisted company debt ratio by 14%. The following year (2009) listed company's debt ratio fell by 11%, and for unlisted companies, it increased by 3%. There was the abnormal increase in the ratio of 194% for listed companies and only 14% increase for unlisted companies in 2010. The following year (2011) the debt ratio for listed companies rose 12 % and 1% decrease for unlisted companies. In 2012 debt to equity ratio increased by 22% (listed companies) and decreased by 65% (Unlisted companies). These variations are due to characteristics of individual companies. The following year (2013), debt ratio for listed companies decreased by 65% and while the ratio for unlisted companies shrank by 1%. The last year (2014) listed companies had a reduction in debt ratio by 10% as compared to an increase of 18% for the unlisted companies.

Table 4:4: Trend Analysis: Debt- Ratio

Year	Listed Companies		Unlisted Companies	
	Mean	% Change	Mean	% Change
2007	0.55		1.89	
2008	0.8	45%	1.63	-14%
2009	0.71	-11%	1.68	3%
2010	2.09	194%	1.91	14%
2011	2.35	12%	1.9	-1%
2012	2.86	22%	1.15	-65%
2013	0.99	-65%	1.14	-1%
2014	0.89	-10%	1.34	18%

Source: Researcher 2017

Figure 4.2 Debt Ratio of Tanzania Companies

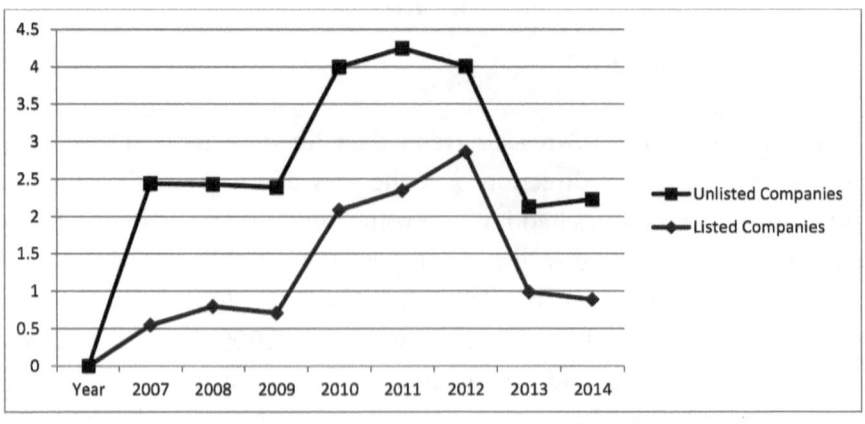

Source: Researcher 2017

Degree of Leverage

Research findings as depicted in Table 4.5 explain the degree of leverage between listed and unlisted companies. The results on 53 observations of debt to equity ratio indicate that listed companies had mean (SD) scores of 0.465(0.236) with minimum and maximum value of 0.015 and 1.08 respectively. However, results for unlisted companies show that the mean value of debt to equity ratio for 213 observations was 0.467 with standard deviation of 0.291 and minimum and maximum value of 0.000 and 1.604 respectively. The finding reveal that listed companies had on average of higher mean scores as compared to lower mean scores of unlisted companies. These results mean suggest that debts of listed companies represent 46% of total equity as compared to 47% of the unlisted companies. The results suggest that all companies have almost the same dependence on debts on financing their business operations, however unlisted companies borrow more and they have less options of using equity to fund their business operations as compared to listed companies.

The results for listed companies show that debt ratio mean value on 53 observations was 1.660 with standard deviation of 3.321 and minimum and maximum value of 0.000 and 15.01 respectively. However, results for unlisted companies show that the mean value of debt ratio for 213 observations was 1.651 with standard deviation of 2.254 and minimum and maximum value of 0.000 and 12.54 respectively. These results suggest that listed companies have more assets to cover the outstanding liabilities than their counterparts. It can also be argued that the listing companies in Tanzania has more equity as compared to unlisted companies because they are constrained to maintain a certain minimum amount of capital by the stock exchange before obtaining the listing status while unlisted company they are not required to keep any minimum amount of capital. From the research findings it shows that listed companies have higher mean values in equity of Tshs 100,518,384m the minimum capital required for stock listing in Tanzania is Tshs 500m which leads to listed companies to have higher mean scores in equity.

Table 4.5: Degree of Leverage of Listed and Unlisted Companies

Construct	Variable	Listed	Unlisted
Debt to Equity	Mean	0.465	0.466
	Median	0.397	0.420
	Standard Deviation	0.236	0.291
	Min	0.015	0.000
	Maximum	1.08	1.604
	Observation	53	213
Debt Ratio	Mean	1.660	1.651
	Median	0.618	0.716
	Standard Deviation	3.321	2.254
	Min	0.000	0.000
	Maximum	15.01	12.54
	Observation	53	213

Source: Research Data 2017

4.3.3 Hypothesis Testing

The aim of testing Hypothesis one is to examine if there are any significance differences between the leverage of listed and unlisted companies in Tanzania.

Hypothesis 1

H1: 1. There is a significance difference in gearing among listed and unlisted companies in Tanzania

We test the hypothesis (H1) to understand if the leverage ratios between listed and unlisted are significantly different and we use t-test to analyze the data. The results of the test below (Table 4.4) show that the debt to equity ratios among the two group of companies in Tanzania are significant different (df 264, t-=-0.46) p=0.965) suggesting that unlisted companies are likely to use more debts as the way of financing their business activities than the listed companies. These results confirm Pagano et al. (1998) propositions that listed firms have less debt as compared to non-listed and therefore less debt-dependent meaning that listed companies have more equity options than the unlisted companies. We also know that market equity is readily available to listed companies. Furthermore, the results reveal statistical differences in debt ratio among listed and unlisted companies (DF 264 t=0.581, p=0.961 suggesting those companies not listed in DSE opt for more debts to meet their assets financing needs as compared to listed companies. The above findings lead to the conclusion that the degree of leverage differs among Tanzanian companies and therefore we can accept the Null hypothesis (H1).

Table 4.6: T-tests between Listed and Unlisted Companies Capital Structure

Company	Debt to Equity Ratio	Debt Ratio
Listed Company	0.465	.1.660
Unlisted Company	0.467	.1.651
t-statistics	-0.046	0.581
df	264	264
Sig(2-tailed)	0.965	0.961

Source: Researcher Data 2017

4.3.4 Discussions on Research Findings

Study findings of the research question one as discussed above indicate that there is a significance difference in leverage between Companies in Tanzania. The study suggest that unlisted companies have higher mean (SD) scores as compared to listed companies with lower mean (SD) scores. Unlisted companies tend to use more debts than the listed companies which have more access to equity funds. The study suggests that the unlisted companies in Tanzania depend more on debts as they have difficult of raising funds through equity issues. The possible reasons for these difficulties is because of the inability of these companies to meet the difficult listing conditions in Tanzania. Majority of the unlisted companies do not meet the minimum capital requirement required for stock listing and therefore cannot obtain equity funds. This means the pecking order theory is relevant for Tanzanian companies as that listed companies are using more of their retained funds and thereafter using equity funds, debts being the last resort of financing their business operations. However, both companies were using debts almost at the slightest difference to fund their business operations. Despite the fact that the sample used in this study might be small to represent all unlisted companies in Tanzania it is evident that the sample is quite sufficient to represent the companies in Tanzania and our findings represent the actual practice of both companies. The results are suggesting that unlisted companies in Tanzania cannot easily access funding through equity but listed companies have both the option of using debts as well as access funding through equity. These findings are contrary to similar to study by Bashar et al. (2015) study which found that the leverage ratio of listed Jordanian firms was significantly lower than that of the non-listed companies. The study by Hall and Jorgensen (2015) confirmed that listed companies did have less debt. On the other side, study by Andani and Al-Hassan (2013) in Ghana gives contrary findings to our findings as it reveals that there leverage of companies is not significantly different between the two groups of companies. This study is also similar to findings of Abhor (2008) who found that listed companies and unlisted companies leverage were not significant different.

4.3.5. Conclusions

The aim of the first research objective was to establish the degree of leverage between listed and unlisted companies in Tanzania. The findings give evidence that there is a significance difference between listed companies and unlisted companies in terms of their leverage. The leverage of unlisted companies is slightly at higher level as compared to that of the listed companies. These differences in leverage between listed and unlisted companies can be explained by various factors, one of them being the inability of unlisted companies to access funds through stock exchange. Majority of unlisted companies in Tanzania are small and they almost affected by inability to meet the listing conditions and costs hence forced to depend on debts to finance their business operations. Listed companies have two options for raising their capital structure and they are likely to minimize their level of borrowing as they are able to rise their funding through equity. Some of the unlisted companies in Tanzania have the capacity to meet conditions for listing which enables them to raise funds through equity but fear of shareholders' diluting the ownership of their companies forces these companies (majority of them being private companies) not to pursue listing options for capital raising through equity. In order to encourage unlisted companies in Tanzania to raise funds through equity funding listing conditions have to be reviewed so as to encourage majority of private companies to be listed in stock exchange. Companies should also be encouraged to seek for alternative methods of financing their capital structure need apart from debt financing. At the same time the research recommends for flexible listing conditions to enable more Tanzanian companies to have easy access to equity funding.

4.4. Research Findings: The influence of Liquidity on Company Leverage

The following section presents the descriptive statistics on liquidity of Tanzanian companies (listed and Unlisted), hypothesis testing (H2), discussion of the research findings consistency with previous studies, conclusions and recommendations. We restate specific research question two here under "To what extent company liquidity influence the leverage of Tanzanian Companies? We present below the detailed findings:

4.4.1 Summary statistics

The results under table 4.7 show various statistical indicators of liquidity characteristics of both listed and listed companies. As far as liquidity is concerned which was measured using the current ratio, the results show that unlisted companies had higher mean (SD)scores of 4.89(19.8) with minimum value of 0 and maximum value of 248.56 as compared to lower mean value of 1.83 and standard deviation of 1.28 of the listed companies with minimum and maximum value of 0.27 and 7.31 respectively. The Maximum value of liquidity for unlisted companies seem to be extreme possibly due to the characteristics of the unlisted companies in holding current assets. These findings show that unlisted companies were more capable of meeting their current maturing obligations by using the most liquid resources as compared to listed companies.

Table 4.7: Descriptive statistics of Liquidity Ratios

Variable	Listed Company	Unlisted Company
Mean	1.83	4.89
Median	1.284	19.79
Standard Deviation	1.284	19.79
Minimum	0.27	0
Maximum	7.31	248.5
Observation	53	213

Source: Researcher 2017

Trend analysis of Liquidity Ratios

Table 4.8 and figure 2reveals trend data for current ratios of the listed and unlisted companies between year 2007 and 2014. In 2007 unlisted companies had higher mean score (SD) in current ratio of 2.35(2.028) as compared to 1.94(1.09) of that of listed companies. In 2008 the current ratio of listed companies increased by 1% compared to increase of unlisted company current ratio by 7%. The following year (2009) listed companies' current ratio fell by 11%, and for unlisted companies, it increased by 38%. The following year (2010) the current ratio for listed companies decreased by 4 % and 58% increase for unlisted companies. In 2011 current ratio increased by 2% (listed companies) and decreased by 37% (Unlisted companies). These variations are due to characteristics of individual companies. The following year (2012), current ratio for listed companies increased by 44% and current ratio for unlisted companies shrank by 26%. The last year (2014) indicates an abnormal decrease in the current ratio of 391% for listed companies and only 301% decrease for unlisted companies in 2014. These abnormal variations are explained by the individual characteristic of the companies as well.

Table 4.8 Trend analysis of Current Ratios (2007-2014)

Year	Listed Companies		Unlisted Companies	
	Mean (SD)	% change	Mean (SD)	% Change
2007	1.94 (1.09)	-	2.35(2.028)	-
2008	1.96 (1.093)	1%	2.53(2.475)	7%

2009	1.77(0.991)	-11%	4.07(9.03)	38%
2010	1.71(0.96)	-4%	9.73(39.57)	58%
2011	1.75(0.97)	2%	7.11(25.09)	-37%
2012	2.16(1.44)	19%	3.48(6.25)	-104%
2013	3.88(6.44)	44%	2.77(3.20)	-26%
2014	0.79(0.455)	-391%	0.69(0.69)	-301%

Source: Researcher 2017

The figure below (Figure 4.3) is the graphical representation of the current ratios of both listed and unlisted companies for the period between year 2007 and year 2017. The graph of unlisted companies depicts that overall the current ratios for the unlisted companies was higher throughout the period of study except in the last two years.

Figure 4.3. Tanzanian Companies Current Ratios (Year 2007-2014)

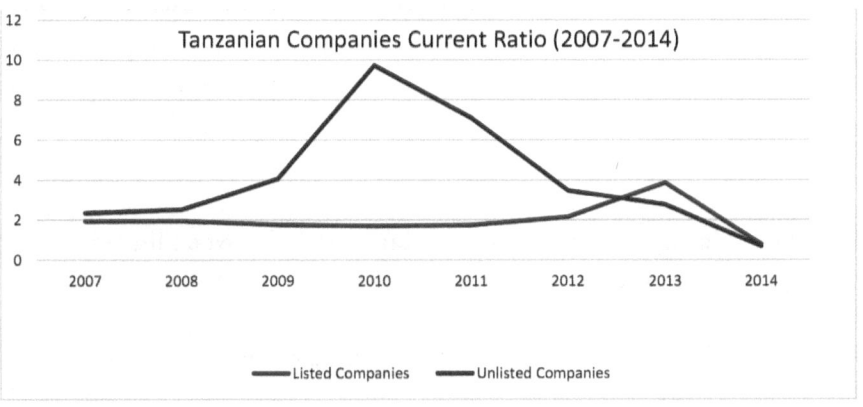

Source: Researcher 2017

Multicloneriarity Tests

This study adopts the Variance inflation factor (VIF) to check if there is any multicolliearnty problem between the main variable of the regression model (Gujarati 2003). In case the VIF results indicate a value above 10 then it is likely that there is multicollinearity problem in the study variables. VIF measures the extent to which actual disparity differs from total disparity. Multicollinearity tests presented under table 4.9 are likely not to present any problem (Neter et al 1983). Based on the regression model with variance inflation factor the results show all models VIF was less than 10.

Table 4.9: Regression Model with Variance Inflation Factor

Model	Regression Model	VIF
Model 1	DEBT RATIO i, t = ß0+ ß1 (CR i, t) + ß2 (Current Ratio i, t) + e	1.000
Model 2	DEBT TO EQUITY i, t = ß0+ ß1 (CR i, t) + ß2 (Current Ratio i, t) +e	1.000

Source: Researcher 2017

4.4.2. Hypothesis testing

We test the hypothesis(H2) to understand if liquidity is negatively related to leverage. We assume current ratio to be the measure of liquidity and debt ratio and debt to equity ratio to measure leverage. We use regression analysis and Pearson Correlation to test the hypothesis. We re-state the hypothesis hereunder

H2: There is a significant negative relationship between liquidity and leverage of Tanzanian Companies

We also test the minor hypotheses re- stated here under

H: 2a: There is a significant negative relationship between liquidity and debt to equity ratio
H: 2b: There is a significant negative relationship between liquidity and debt ratio

Correlation Analysis

Table below (Table 4.10) presents the results of hypothesis two. The tests results indicate that a significant negative correlation of (-0.133*) exists between current ratio and debt to equity ratio at significant level of 0.05. Correlation results also indicate existence of negative correlation of -0.085 between current ratio and debt ratio which is not significant. We can therefore We therefore accept the Null hypothesis (H2a: There is a significant negative relationship between liquidity and debt to equity ratio).

Table 4.10: Correlation between current ratio and Leverage

Variable	Liquidity	Debt to Equity Ratio	Debt Ratio
Liquidity	1.000		
Debt to Equity Ratio	-.133*	1.000	
Debt Ratio	-.085	.658**	1.000
*. Correlation is significant at the 0.05 level (2-tailed).			
**. Correlation is significant at the 0.01 level (2-tailed).			

Source: Researcher 2017

Regression Analysis: Company Liquidity and Debt to Equity Ratio

The regression analysis discussed below examined the relationship between company liquidity and leverage of listed and unlisted companies as measured by debt to equity ratio. We consider liquidity (Current ratio) as independent variable and debt to equity ratio as dependent variable. The table below (Table 4.11) show (R^2) Value of 0.133 which means that 13.30% of the variation in debt to equity ratio is explained by the independent variable (Liquidity). At the same time, Durban Watson statistic (0.674) shows that there is lack of autocorrelation between the model errors.

$$D/ERATIO_{i,t} = ß0 + ß2\,(LIQ_{i,t}) + e \qquad \text{Model 1}$$

Table 4: 11- Variation of the Regression Model – Debt to Equity

Model	R	R Square	Adjusted R Square	Std. Error of the Estimate	Durbin-Watson
1	.133ª	0.018	0.014	.278	0.674
a. Predictors: (Constant), Liquidity					
b. Dependent Variable: Debt to Equity Ratio					

Source: Researcher 2017

According to table 4.12. ANOVA results show a P-Value of 0.029 which (means p-value<0.005) is the above fitted model at 0.000 helps us to conclude that our regression model results are significantly better prediction of company leverage (debt to Equity Ratio) rather than using the mean value of capital structure determinants.

Table 4.12. ANOVA: Company Liquidity and Debt to Equity Ratio

Model		Sum of Squares	df	Mean Square	F	Sig.
1	Regression	373	1	373	4.816	.029[b]
	Residual	20.606	266	5.884		
	Total	20.979	267			

a. Dependent Variable: Debt to Equity Ratio
b. Predictors: (Constant), Liquidity

Source: Researcher 2017

By analyzing the results of Model 2 below (Table 4.13) show liquidity having negative results (Beta=-0.02) with (sig=0.029) significance level means that liquidity negatively impacts debt to equity ratio and this leads to the conclusion of accepting the Null hypothesis (H1;1a) that there is negative relationship between liquidity and debt to equity ratio.

Table 4.13 Regression- Liquidity and Debt to Equity Ratio Multicolliearnity tests -Coefficients

Model		Unstandardized Coefficients		Standardized Coefficients	t	Sig.	Collinearity Statistics	
		B	Std. Error	Beta			Tolerance	VIF
1	(Constant)	.474	0.17		27.110	000		
	Liquidity	-002	001	-0133	-2.195	029	1.000	1.000

a. Dependent Variable: Debt to Equity Ratio

Source: Researcher 2017

Regression Analysis: Company Liquidity and Debt Ratio

The regression analysis discussed below (Table 4.14) examined the relationship between company liquidity and leverage of listed and unlisted companies. We consider liquidity (Current ratio) as independent variable and debt ratio as dependent variable. The table below (Table 4.12) show (R2) Value of 0.07 which means that 7% of the variation in debt to equity ratio is explained by the independent variable (Liquidity). At the same time, Durban Watson statistic (0.661) shows that there is lack of autocorrelation between the model errors.

$$D/RATIO_{i,t} = ß0 + ß2 (LIQ_{i,t}) + e \qquad \text{Model (2)}$$

Table 4.14 - Variation of the Regression Model – Debt ratio

Model	R	R Square	Adjusted R Square	Std. Error of the Estimate	Durbin-Watson
2	.085^a	0.07	0.003	2.456	0.661

a. Predictors: (Constant), Liquidity
b. Dependent Variable: Debt Ratio

Source: Researcher 2017

According to table 4.15 ANOVA results show a P-Value of 0.166 which (means p-value<0.005) is the above fitted model at 0.000 helps us to conclude that our regression model results is significantly better prediction of company leverage (debt to Equity Ratio) rather than using the mean value of capital structure determinants.

Table 4.15. ANOVA: Company Liquidity and Debt Ratio

Model		Sum of Squares	df	Mean Square	F	Sig.
2	Regression	373	1	11.664	1.933	.166^b
	Residual	1605.119	266	6.034		
	Total	1616.783	267			

a. Dependent Variable: Debt Ratio
b. Predictors: (Constant), Liquidity

Source: Researcher Data 2017

By analyzing the results of Model 6 above (Table 4.16) show liquidity having negative results (Beta= -0.012) with (sig=0.0166) significance level means that liquidity negatively impacts debt ratio and this leads to the conclusion of accepting the Null hypothesis (H1:1a) that there is negative relationship between liquidity and debt ratio.

Table 4.16: -Regression- Liquidity and Debt Ratio Multicolliearnity tests -Coefficients

Model		Unstandardized Coefficients		Standardized Coefficients	t	Sig.	Collinearity Statistics	
		B	Std. Error	Beta			Tolerance	VIF
2	(Constant)	1.695	0.154		10.977	000		
	Liquidity	-012	006	-085	-1.390	166	1.000	1.000
a. Dependent Variable: Debt Ratio								

Source: Researcher 2017

4.4.3 Discussions on Research Findings

Research findings have revealed that there is negative relationship between liquidity and leverage among Tanzanian companies. Liquidity is negatively related to both debt to equity ratio (H2:2a) and debt ratio (H2:2b). The findings of this study suggest that majority of Tanzanian companies are small and seem to have inadequate liquidity to finance their business activities by using internal funds hence majority of them will have to opt to use more debts to finance their activities. It is also evident that in Tanzania there are few companies that have access to equity funds through listing as the conditions easily excludes those companies with lower liquidity. The findings of this study do match with only few findings of the previous studies in other countries. Mahmood and Mansor (2008) studied the listed companies in Malyisia to understand the relationship between liquidity and company leverage and found that there was a negative relationship between liquidity and debt levels. Ahmad and Aris (2015) study of capital structure determinants in service industry in Bursa Malaysia indicated a significant negative impact of liquidity on leverage. Negative relationship between liquidity and leverage is consistent to the prediction of the pecking order. Pecking order predicts a negative relationship between liquidity and company leverage.

The findings of this study are not consistent to the Trade-off theory which predicts a positive relationship between liquidity and leverage and are not consistent with other previous studies. Sibilkov (2009) investigation on the effect of liquid assets on capital structure found that liquidity was positively correlated to leverage. Olayinka (2011) study in Nigeria companies concluded that leverage and liquidity are positively correlated. Another study on capital structure by Khalay (2013) in Malaysian companies found that there is a significant positive relationship between liquidity ratios and leverage. These findings were consistent with the trade- off theory. The study of Croatian's companies by Sarlija and Hare (2012) revealed that there are statistically significant relationships between liquidity and leverage ratios. However, the relationship between liquidity and long-term leverage was weaker than the relationship between liquidity and short-term leverage.

4.4.4. Conclusions

By virtue of the research findings, the testing of the hypotheses (H2:2a and H2:2b) reveal that there is a negative relationship between company liquidity and company leverage as measured by debt ratio and debt to equity ratio. This finding suggests that as liquidity of Tanzanian companies increase less debts is used to finance business operations. Therefore, we can conclude that higher liquidity companies in Tanzania would prefer using internal funds instead of borrowing.

These findings do suggest that the pecking order assumptions are more relevant in case of Tanzanian companies. Based on the findings of this study it is recommended to Tanzanian companies' managers n to improve their liquidity in order to avoid the problem of relying on debts to finance their business operations. Increase in liquidity on the other side is likely to help Tanzanian companies to increase their profitability over time and hence be able to meet one of the listing conditions in Tanzania and at the end have access to equity funds.

However, only one variable (Current ratio) was used as the measure of liquidity against two variables of dependent variable (debt ratio and debt equity ratio). Therefore, conducting a further research based on use of more variables indicators of liquidity and leverage could result into different findings and conclusions. The study was also limited in terms of sample characteristics as few companies participated in the study due to difficulties of obtaining financial statements from many private companies. The secrecy nature of private companies leads to difficulties of more companies participating in the study. Given the fact that one is able to increase the sample of private unlisted companies to participate in the study, the likely results might indicate a different relationship between company liquidity and leverage.

4.5 Research Findings: The Influence of Profitability and Company Leverage

In this section we present the descriptive statistics on the company profitability of both listed and unlisted companies as well the hypothesis testing, discussion of the research findings consistency with previous studies and capital structure theories, conclusions and recommendations. We restate specific research question three here under *"To what extent company profitability influence the leverage of Tanzanian Companies?* The results are presented hereunder:

4.5.1 Summary Statistics

According to table 4.17 various statistical indicators show the characteristics of profitability indicators by both listed and listed companies. In terms of profitability which is measured by return on equity (ROE), unlisted companies have higher mean of 4.89 and standard deviation of 26.09 with minimum and maximum value of -0.82 and 330.4 respectively in 213 observations. Listed companies have lower mean value of 0.54 and standard deviation of (26.09) with minimum and maximum value 0f – 0.16 and 2.72 respectively in 53 observations. These results mean that unlisted companies' shareholders were able to receive higher return for every single shilling invested as compared to listed companies. However, the minimum negative value by both companies means that some companies were making losses.

Table 4.17: Descriptive statistics of Return on Equity (ROE)

Variable	Listed Company	Unlisted Company
Mean	0.44	4.89
Median		
Standard Deviation	0.54	26.09
Minimum	-0.16	-0.82
Maximum	2.72	330
Observation	53	213

Source: Researcher 2017

On return on assets (ROA) the results (Table 4.18) show that unlisted companies have higher mean value of 1.37 and standard deviation of 10.28 in 212 observations with minimum and maximum value of -0.63 and 139.90 respectively. The listed companies had mean value of 0.23 and standard deviation of 0.3 in 53 observations with minimum and maximum value of -0.11 and 1.49 respectively. The negative minimum value of ROA is explained by company characteristics in the sample and signifies that some companies were operating in losses in some years. These results mean that unlisted companies assets generated more return than the assets by listed companies. Since ROA is assumed to be the measure of company's ability to generate capital internally (Kester 1986, Pandey et al 2000) these results show that unlisted companies generated more return internally than the listed companies.

Table 4.18: Descriptive statistics of Return on Assets (ROA)

Variable	Listed Company	Unlisted Company
Mean	0.23	1.37
Median		
Standard Deviation	0.3	10.28
Minimum	-0.11	-0.63
Maximum	1.49	139.90

Observation	53	213

Source: Researcher 2017

Trend Analysis

Table 4.19 and figure 4.5 reveals trend data for return on assets (ROE) of the listed and unlisted companies between year 2007 and 2014. The table below indicates that unlisted companies had higher mean score (SD) of 13.25(58.7) as compared to 0.98(0.77) of that of listed companies. In 2008 the return on equity (ROE) of listed companies decreased by 44% compared to decrease of unlisted company return on equity by 49%. The following year (2009) listed companies return on equity fell by 38%, and for unlisted companies, it decreased by 59%.

The following year (2010) the return on equity ratio for listed companies decreased by 32 % and 65% decrease for unlisted companies. In 2011 current ratio increased by 22% (listed companies) and increased by 13% (Unlisted companies). These variations are due to characteristics of individual companies. The following year (2012) the return on equity for listed companies increased by 36% and return on equity for unlisted companies shrank by 74%. The last year (2014) indicates a decrease in the current ratio by 60% for listed companies with no change in return in equity for unlisted companies in 2014. These variations in return on equity are explained by the individual characteristic of the companies as well as well as unknown factors not investigated by this study.

Table 4.19: Trend Analysis of Return on Equity (ROE)

Year	Listed Companies		Unlisted Companies	
	Mean (SD)	% Change	Mean (SD)	% Change
2007	0.98 (0.77)		13.23(58.7)	
2008	0.55(0.56)	-44%	6.73(26.71)	-49%
2009	0.34(0.35)	-38%	2.75(10.8)	-59%
2010	0.23(0.22)	-32%	0.97(3.96)	-65%
2011	0.28(0.281)	22%	1.10(4.51)	13%
2012	0.38(0.44)	36%	0.29(0.715)	-74%

2013	0.89(1.22)	134%	0.09(0.691)	-69%
2014	0.36(0.22)	-60%	0.09(0.223)	0%

Source: Researcher 2017

Figure 4.4 depicts the graphical representation of the variation in return on equity (ROE) of both companies from year 2007 t0 2017. Unlisted companies had higher Mean score between year 2007 and 2011 but lower score from 2012 to 2014 as compared to listed companies which had higher mean scores since year 2012 to 2014. This study has not been able to establish the reasons for these variations.

Figure 4.4: Return on Equity for Listed and Unlisted Companies (2007-2014).

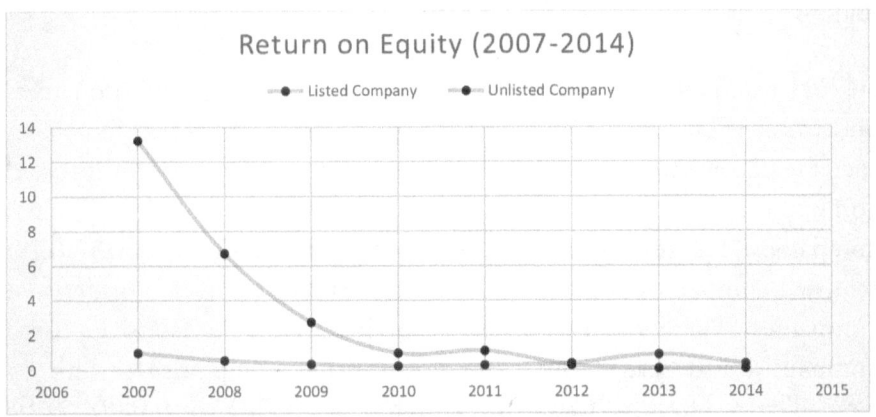

Source: Researcher 2017

As far as Return on assets is concerned Table 4.20 and figure 4.6 reveals trend data for return on assets (ROA) of the listed and unlisted companies between year 2007 and 2014. The return on Assets (ROA) below show that unlisted companies had higher mean score (SD) of 0.79 (2.15) as compared to 0.69(0.61) of that of listed companies. This means that assets of unlisted companies generated more returns as compared to listed companies' assets. In year 2008 results show that unlisted companies had higher mean score (SD) of 0.68(1.48) as compared to lower mean score (SD) of 0.33(0.31) of the listed companies. This is a decrease of 52% in ROA for listed companies compared to decrease of

14% for unlisted companies. These results show that the capability of listed companies to generate returns declined higher than the one of the listed companies. In year 2009 results show that unlisted companies had higher mean score (SD) of 0.44(1.91) as compared to lower mean score (SD) of 0.21(0.19) of the listed companies. This is a decrease of 35% in ROA for listed companies compared to decrease of 36% for unlisted companies. These results show that the capability of listed companies to generate returns declined higher than the one of the listed companies.

The following year (2010) the return on assets results show mean scores (SD) of 0.21(0.19) for listed companies and 0.29(1.08) for unlisted companies. This shows that ratio for listed companies decreased by 29 % and 34 % decrease for unlisted companies.

In 2011 results show mean scores (SD) of 0.17(0.19) for listed companies and Mean (SD) scores of 0.38(1.33) for unlisted companies. This is an increase of 13% for listed companies) and increased by 31% for unlisted companies. These variations are due to characteristics of individual companies. The results for 2012 show a higher mean (SD) of 0.17(0.19) by listed companies as compared to mean (SD) of 0.15(0.25) of unlisted companies. There was no % change in the return on assets for listed companies and return on assets for unlisted companies shrank by 61%. The results for 2013 show a higher mean (SD) of 0.08(0.17) by listed companies as compared to mean (SD) of 0.06(0.098) of unlisted companies. These results show a decrease in the ROA by 53% for listed companies and 60% by that of unlisted companies. Final year results (2014) show higher mean (SD) score of 0.02(0.06) of unlisted companies against mean (SD) of 0.01(0.09) of that of listed companies. These results show a decrease in the ROA by 88% for listed companies and 67% by that of unlisted companies. These variations in return on Assets are explained by the individual characteristic of the companies as well as well as unknown factors not investigated by this study.

Table 4.20: Trend Analysis of Return on Equity (ROE)

Year	Listed Companies Mean (SD)	% Change	Unlisted Companies Mean (SD)	% Change
2007	0.69(0.61)		0.79(2.15)	
2008	0.33(0.31)	-52%	0.68(1.91)	-14%
2009	0.21(0.19)	-36%	0.44(1.48)	-35%
2010	0.15(0.15)	-29%	0.29(1.08)	-34%
2011	0.17(0.19)	13%	0.38(1.33)	31%
2012	0.17(0.19)	0%	0.15(.25)	-61%
2013	0.08(0.17)	-53%	0.06(.098)	-60%
2014	0.01(0.09)	-88%	0.02(0.06)	-67%

Source: Researcher 2017

Figure 4.5 depicts the graphical representation of the variation in return on Assets (ROA) of both companies from year 2007 t0 2014. Unlisted companies had higher Mean score between year 2007 and 2011 but lower score from 2012 to 2014 as compared to listed companies which had higher mean scores since year 2012 to 2014. This study has not been able to establish the reasons for these variations

Figure 4.5: Return on Assets for Listed and Unlisted Companies (2007-2014).

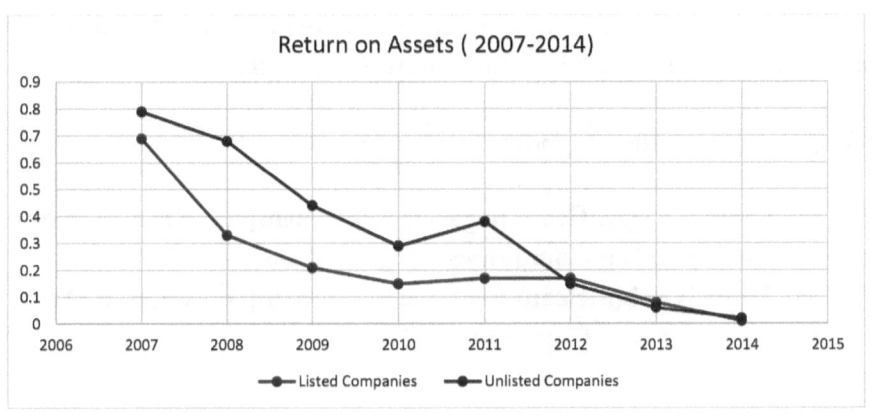

Source: Researcher 2017

Multicloneriarity Tests

This study adopts the Variance inflation factor (VIF) to check if there is any multicolliearnity problem between the main variable of the regression model (Gujarati 2003). VIF measures the relationship between actual disparity and total depravity. Multicollinearity tests presented under table 4.20 are likely not to present any problem (Neter et al 1983) Based on the regression model with variance inflation factor the results show all models VIF was less than 10.

Table 4.21: Regression Model with Variance Inflation Factor

Model	Regression Model	VIF
Model 3	DEBT RATIO i, t = ß0+ ß1 (ROE i, t) + ß1 (ROA i, t) + e	6.437
Model 4	DEBT TO EQUITY i, t = ß0+ ß1 (ROE i, t) + ß1 (ROA i, t) + e	6.437

Source: Researcher 2017

4.5.2 Hypothesis testing

We test the relationship between profitability and company leverage by using the Pearson correlation analysis and regression analysis. We re-state the hypothesis three hereunder

H3: There is a significant negative relationship between company profitability and leverage of Tanzanian Companies

We also test the minor hypotheses re- stated here under

H3: 3a: There is a significant negative relationship between ROE and leverage of Tanzanian Companies
H3: 3b: There is a significant negative relationship between ROA and leverage of Tanzanian Companies

Correlation Analysis

Correlation analysis is performed (Table 4.22) to show the relationship between profitability ratios (as independent variable) namely return on

Equity (ROE) and return on Assets (ROA) and leverage as dependent variable measured by debt ratio and debt to equity ratio. The results show that there is a significant positive correlation between return on equity and debt to equity ratio 0.101 and there is significant positive correlation of 0.086 between return on equity and debt ratio. Correlation is significant at the 0.01 level. We therefore reject the minor Null hypothesis (H2:2a: There is a negative relationship between ROE and debt Ratio) and conclude that there is a positive relationship between company profitability and leverage of Tanzanian companies.

Correlation results also shows a positive relationship between return on assets and debt to equity ratio (0.034) and shows a positive correlation of 0.015 between return on assets and debt ratio. Correlation is also significant at 0.01 level We also reject the minor Null Hypothesis (H2;2b: There is a negative relationship between ROA and leverage of Tanzanian Companies). We can therefore conclude that there is positive relationship between profitability and leverage of Tanzanian companies (H2) as measured by debt to equity ratio and debt ratio.

Table 4.22: Correlation Analysis between Profitability ratios and Leverage Ratios

Variable	**Return on Equity**	**Return on Assets**	**Debt to Equity Ratio**	**Debt Ratio**
Return on Equity	1.000			
Return on Assets	.919**	1.000		
Debt to Equity Ratio	0.101	0.034	1.000	
Debt Ratio	0.086	0.015	.658**	1.000
**. Correlation is significant at the 0.01 level (2-tailed).				

Source: Researcher 2017

Regression Analysis: Company Profitability and Debt to Equity Ratio

The regression analysis discussed below examined the relationship between company liquidity and leverage of listed and unlisted companies as measured by debt to equity ratio. We consider liquidity (Current ratio) as independent variable and debt to equity ratio as dependent variable.

The table below (Table 4.23) show (R^2) Value of 0.032 which means that 3% of the variation in debt to equity ratio is explained by Return assets and Return on Assets (ROA). At the same time, Durban Watson statistic (0.667) shows that there is lack of autocorrelation between the model errors.

$$D/ERATIO_{i,t} = ß0 + ß1 (ROE_{i,t}) + ß2 (ROA_{i,t}) + e \qquad \text{Model 3}$$

Table 4: 23 - Variation of the Regression Model – Debt to Equity

Model	R	R Square	Adjusted R Square	Std. Error of the Estimate	Durbin-Watson
3	0.179[a]	0.032	0.025	.276	0.0667

a. Predictors: (Constant), Return on Equity, Return on Assets
b. Dependent Variable: Debt to Equity Ratio

Source: Researcher 2017

According to table 4.24. ANOVA results show a P-Value of 0.013 which is the above fitted model at 0.000 helps us to conclude that our regression model results are significantly better prediction of company leverage (debt to Equity Ratio) rather than using the mean value of profitability indicators (Return on Assets and Return on Equity)

Table 4.24. ANOVA: Company Profitability and Debt to Equity Ratio

Model		Sum of Squares	df	Mean Square	F	Sig.
3	Regression	668	1	334	4.377	.013[b]
	Residual	20.151	264	0.076		
	Total	20,819	266			
	a. Dependent Variable: Debt to Equity Ratio					
	b. Predictors: (Constant), Return on Assets, Return on Equity					

Source: Researcher 2017

By analyzing the results of Model 2 below (Table 4.25) show profitability (ROE) having positive results (Beta=-0.05) with (sig=0.004) significance level means that return on equity positively impacts debt to equity ratio and this leads to the conclusion of accepting the Null hypothesis (H1a) that there is positive relationship between profitability and debt to equity ratio. However, results also shows ROA having negative results (Beta=-0.11) with (sig=0.015) significance level means that return on equity negatively impacts debt to equity ratio.

Table 4.25 Regression- Profitability and Debt to Equity Ratio Multicolliearnity tests -Coefficients

Coefficients							
Model	Unstandardized Coefficients		Standardized Coefficients	t	Sig.	Collinearity Statistics	
	B	Std. Error	Beta			Tolerance	VIF
3 (Constant)	.459	.017		26.857	.000		
Return on Equity	.005	.002	.446	2.904	.004	.155	6.437
Return on Assets	-.011	.005	-.376	-2.447	.015	.155	6.437
a. Dependent Variable: Debt to Equity Ratio							

Source: Researcher 2017

Regression Analysis: Company Profitability and Debt Ratio

Table 4.26 below explain the results of the regression analysis that determines the relationship between profitability and leverage. The independent variables are return on Assets (ROA) and Return on equity (ROE) and the dependent variable is debt ratio. The results below show (R^2) Value of 0.033 which means that 3% of the variation in debt to ratio is explained by Return equity (ROE) and Return on Assets (ROA). The autocorrelation tests, Durban Watson statistic (0.710) shows that there is lack of autocorrelation between the model errors.

$DRATIO_{i,t} = ß0 + ß1\,(ROE_{i,t}) + ß2\,(ROA_{i,t}) + e$ Model 4

Table 4: 26 - Variation of the Regression Model – Debt to Equity

Model	R	R Square	Adjusted R Square	Std. Error of the Estimate	Durbin-Watson
4	0.182[a]	0.033	0.026	2.416	0.710

a. Predictors: (Constant), Return on Equity, Return on Assets
b. Dependent Variable: Debt to Ratio

Source: Researcher 2017

The table below (Table 4.27) shows. ANOVA results with P-Value of 0.012. This is the above fitted model at 0.000 hence it helps us to conclude that our regression model results are significantly better prediction of company leverage (debt Ratio) rather than using the mean value of profitability indicators (Return on Assets and Return on Equity)

Table 4.27: ANOVA: Company Profitability and Debt Ratio

Model		Sum of Squares	df	Mean Square	F	Sig.
3	Regression	52.818	2	26.409	4.524	.012[b]
	Residual	1540.98	264	5.837		
	Total	1593.803	266			
	a. Dependent Variable: Debt Ratio					
	b. Predictors: (Constant), Return on Assets, Return on Equity					

Source: Researcher 2017

By analyzing the results of Model 4 below (Table 4.28) show profitability (ROE) having positive results (Beta=-0.048) with (sig=0.003) significance level means that return on equity positively impacts debt ratio and this leads to the conclusion of accepting the Null hypothesis (H1a) that there is positive relationship between profitability and debt to equity ratio. However, results also shows ROA having negative results (Beta=-0.109) with (sig=0.008) significance level means that return on assets negatively impacts debt ratio.

Table 4.28 Regression- Profitability and Debt Ratio Multicolliearnity tests -Coefficients

Coefficients								
Model		Unstandardized Coefficients		Standardized Coefficients	t	Sig.	Collinearity Statistics	
		B	Std. Error	Beta			Tolerance	VIF
4	(Constant)	1.589	.149		26.857	.000		
	Return on Equity	.048	.016	.460	2.997	.003	.155	6.437
	Return on Assets	-.109	.041	-.408	-2.654	.008	.155	6.437
a. Dependent Variable: Debt to Ratio								

Source: Researcher 2017

4.5.3 Discussion on Research Findings

The study findings have revealed a positive relationship between profitability (measured by return on equity (ROE) and return on Assets (ROA) and leverage of Tanzanian companies' contrary to the prediction of the pecking order theory and findings of the previous studies but confirming the prediction of the trade- off theory. The prediction of negative relationship between profitability and leverage are on the basis of inclination of profitable companies preferring to use their retained earnings for internal financing instead of using external funding. These predictions do not ignore the assumptions of the Modigliani and Miller (1963) tax model. Where there are high taxes imposed on company's profits, companies would prefer to use debt financing instead of using internal funds in order to take advantage of the tax shield on debt

The study findings suggest that as the profitability of Tanzanian companies increases, these companies do not prefer to use internal sources (retained earnings) to finance their activities instead they prefer using debts. This is completely opposite to the inclination of using the profitability (Retained earnings) to fund the business operations. Tanzanian companies are relying more on debts even those with higher level of profitability because they want to take advtanges of tax benefits as the loan interest expenses becomes allowable expenses hence reducing their tax liabilities.

The findings of this study are in conformance with many previous studies that reveal a negative relationship between profitability and leverage. Myers (1984) found that profitability was negatively correlated to leverage while Sheel (1994) and Wald (199) study indicate that profitability and leverage had negative relationship. Observations by Titman and Wessels (1988) reveal that more profitable companies had lower leverage as compared to less leveraged companies. Other Previous findings by Hall et al (2000), Benan and Dan bolt (2001) and Booth et al (2001) reveal a negative relationship between profitability and leverage supporting the pecking order.

However, the findings of this study confirm the predictions of the tradeoff theory. Trade off theory predicts a positive relationship between profitability and leverage. The theory has assumed that profitable companies would prefer using debts in order to benefit from the tax shield and therefore companies can borrow more. Tax deductability of interest payments encourages to use debts hence that profitable companies will tend to have high level of debts. Studies by Jensen (1992): Ye Zhang (2010) found a positive relationship between profitability and leverage confirming the prediction of the trade-off theory.

4.5.4 Conclusions

The study investigated the relationship between profitability and leverage of Tanzanian companies. The study found that the profitability of unlisted companies was higher than that of the listed companies, though over the study period the profitability indicators (ROA and ROE) of listed companies was declining at higher rate than the ones of the unlisted companies. The study did not establish the reasons for the decline in profitability of Tanzanian companies (ROE and ROA). Therefore, managers of both companies need to study the causes of such major declines and develop strategies to enhance the profitability of their companies.

The study also found positive relationship between profitability and leverage suggesting that majority of Tanzanian companies used debts as the means of financing their business operations. These suggestions are also backed up with the existence of few companies that are listed in the stock exchange that are able to raise funds through equity funds. Further studies are needed to investigate what supportive Policies or strategies are needed in Tanzania to encourage more companies to access funding through equity. The study also used only two measures of profitability namely ROE and ROA were used in this particular study. The use of only 59 companies also limits the conclusions of the findings. Conclusions drawn from this study may imply that if other indicators of profitability and more companies could be used in further studies the results might reveal different findings which may concur on not concur with the predictions of the pecking order or trade off theories.

4.6 Research Findings: The Influence of Tangibility and Company Leverage

This section presents the descriptive statistics on company tangibility of the listed and unlisted companies in Tanzania as well the hypothesis testing, discussion of the research findings on basis of the predictions of the pecking order theory, static trade off theory and previous studies. Finally, we give conclusions and recommendations. We restate specific research question here under ***"To what extent does tangibility influence the leverage of Tanzanian companies as implied by trade off theory and pecking order theory?*** The results are presented hereunder:

4.6.1. Summary Statistics

Table 4.29 shows the characteristic of assets tangibility of both listed and unlisted companies for the period 2007 to 2014. Tangibility was measured by using tangibility ratio (Fixed assets divided by Total Assets). The results show that listed companies have higher mean (SD) score of 0.63 (0.140) with minimum and maximum value of 0 and 1 respectively in 53 observations. Listed companies have mean (SD) core of 0.54(26.09) with minimum and maximum value of 0 and 1 respectively in 53 observations. These results mean that listed companies' shareholders have invested more money in tangible assets as compared to unlisted companies. However, the minimum value of 0 in value by both companies means that some companies have no investment in tangible assets

Table 4:29 Descriptive statistics of Companies Tangibility

Variable	Listed Company	Unlisted Company
Mean	0.63	0.54
Standard Deviation	0.140	0.276
Minimum	0.00	0.00
Maximum	1.000	1.000
Observation	53	213

Source: Researcher 2017

Trend Analysis

Table 4.30 and figure 4.6 shows the trend on fixed assets tangibility of the listed and unlisted companies between year 2007 and 2014. The table below indicates listed companies had higher mean score (SD) of 0.56(0.09) as compared to 0.49(0.14) of that of unlisted companies. This means that listed companies have invested more in tangible fixed assets. The results for 2008 show higher mean (SD) score of 0.60 (0.124) in tangibility by listed companies against mean (SD) score of 0.54(0.289) of the unlisted companies. This shows that in 2008 the tangibility ratio of listed companies increased by 7% compared to an increase 10% for unlisted company. The following year (2009) the results show higher mean (SD) score of 0.60 (0.124) in tangibility by listed companies against mean (SD) score of 0.54(0.289) of the unlisted companies. This shows that in 2008 the tangibility ratio of listed companies increased by 5% compared to an increase 6% for unlisted company.

In year 2010 the results show higher mean (SD) scores of 0.60 (0.124) in tangibility by listed companies against mean (SD) score of 0.54(0.289) of the unlisted companies. This shows that in 2008 the tangibility ratio of listed companies increased by 5% compared to a decrease of 2% for unlisted company. The following year (2011) listed companies had mean (SD) scores of 0.67(0.128) against mean score (SD)scores of 0.52(0.246) of unlisted companies. This shows that tangibility ratio for listed companies increased by 5 % and 4% decrease for unlisted companies.

In year 2012 listed companies had mean (SD) scores of 0.63(0.128) against mean score (SD)scores of 0.52(0.246) of unlisted companies. This shows that tangibility ratio for listed companies increased by 5 % and 4% decrease for unlisted companies. In year 2012 listed companies had mean (SD) scores of 0.67(0.154) against mean score (SD)scores of 0.55(0.246) of unlisted companies. This shows that tangibility ratio for listed companies decreased by 6 % and 6% increase for unlisted companies. The following year (2013) listed companies had mean (SD) scores of fixed assets tangibility of 0.60(0.247) against mean score (SD)scores of 0.59(0.240) of unlisted companies. This shows that tangibility ratio for listed companies decreased by 5 % and increased by 7% for unlisted companies

The final year (2014) listed companies had mean (SD) scores of fixed assets tangibility of 0.78(0.111) against mean score (SD)scores of 0.42(0.003) of unlisted companies. This indicates an increase of 30% for listed companies against a decrease of 29% in tangibility ratio of the unlisted companies. The variation of fixed assets tangibility is explained by the individual characteristic of the companies as well as well as unknown factors not investigated by this study.

Table 4.30: Trend Analysis of Asset Tangibility

	Listed Companies		Unlisted	
Year	Mean (SD)	% Change	Mean (SD)	% Change
2007	0.56(0.092)		0.49(0.314)	
2008	0.60(0.124)	7%	0.54(0.289)	10%
2009	0.63(0.110)	5%	0.57(0.284)	6%
2010	0.64(0.152)	2%	0.54(0.261)	-5%
2011	0.67(0.128)	5%	0.52(0.246)	-4%
2012	0.63(0.154)	-6%	0.55(0.229)	6%
2013	0.60(0.247)	-5%	0.59(0.240)	7%

| 2014 | 0.78(0.111) | 30% | 0.42(.003) | -29% |

Source: Researcher 2017

Figure 4.6 depicts the graphical representation of the variation in tangibility ratio of both companies from year 2007 t0 2017. Listed companies had higher Mean score between year 2007 and 2014 as compared to Unlisted companies which had lower mean scores since year 2012 to 2014. This study has not been able to establish the reasons as to why the listed companies had more assets than the unlisted companies. However, from the literature we can assume that the secrecy nature of most unlisted companies which are private companies can lead to non-disclosure of all financial information.

Figure 4.6: Company Tangibility Ratio (2007-2014).

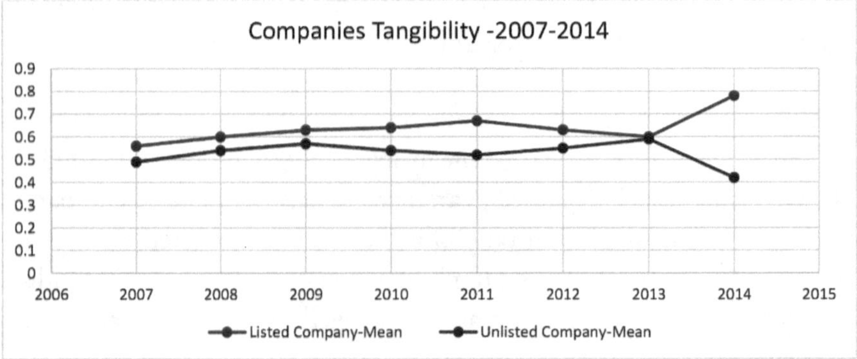

Source: Researcher Data 2017

Multicloneriarity Tests

This study adopts the Variance inflation factor (VIF) to check if there is any multicolliearnity problem between the main variable of the regression model. VIF measures the relationship between actual disparity and total depravity. Based on the regression model with variance inflation factor Results (Table 4.31) was 1.000 which is less than 10 then we conclude to have no multilinearity problem.

Table 4.31; Regression Model with Variance Inflation Factor

Model	Regression Model	VIF
Model 5	DEBT RATIO i, t = ß0+ ß1 (TANG i, t) + e	1.000
Model 6	DEBT TO EQUITY i, t = ß0+ ß1 (TANG i, t) + e	1.000

Source: Researcher 2017

4.6.2. Hypothesis testing

We test the relationship between profitability and company leverage by using the Pearson correlation analysis and regression analysis. We re-state the hypothesis four hereunder;

H4: There is positive relationship between assets tangibility and company leverage

Hypothesis five has another two minor hypotheses stated here under

H: 4a: There is a positive relationship between assets tangibility and debt to equity ratio
H: 4b: There is a positive relationship between assets tangibility and debt ratio

Correlation Analysis

Correlation analysis is performed (Table 4.32) to show the relationship between fixed assets tangibility ratios (as independent variable) and leverage as dependent variable measured by debt ratio and debt to equity ratio. The results show that there is a significant negative correlation of -0.252 between fixed assets tangibility and debt ratio to equity ratio. We therefore reject the minor Null hypothesis (H1a: *There is a significant positive relationship between tangibility and debt to equity ratio*) and conclude that there is negative correlation between fixed assets tangibility and debt to equity ratio. Correlation results also shows a negative relationship between tangibility and debt ratio (-0.106). We also reject the minor Null Hypothesis (H1b: There is a significant positive relationship between tangibility and leverage of Tanzanian Companies). We can therefore conclude that that there is negative relationship between tangibility and leverage of Tanzanian companies (H1) as measured by debt ratio.

Table 4.32: Correlation Analysis – Fixed assets Tangibility and Leverage

Correlations			
	Tangibility	Debt to Equity Ratio	Debt Ratio
Tangibility	1		
Debt to Equity Ratio	-.252**	1	
Debt Ratio	-0.106	.658**	1
**. Correlation is significant at the 0.01 level (2-tailed).			

Source: Researcher 2017

Regression Analysis: Company Tangibility and Debt to Equity Ratio

The regression results below show the relationship between tangibility ratio and leverage of both listed and unlisted companies as measured by debt to equity ratio. We consider Tangibility (Fixed Assets/Total Assets) as independent variable and debt to equity ratio as dependent variable. The table below (Table 4.33) show (R^2) Value of 0.252 which means that 25.2% of the variation in debt to equity ratio is explained by fixed assets Tangibility. At the same time, Durban Watson statistic (0.679) shows that there is lack of autocorrelation between the model errors

$$D/ERATIO_{i,t} = ß0 + ß1\ (Tang_{i,t})) + e\ \text{Model 5}$$

Table 4:33 - Variation of the Regression Model – Debt to Equity

Model	R	R Square	Adjusted R Square	Std. Error of the Estimate	Durbin-Watson
1	0.252ª	0.064	0.060	.272	0.0679
a. Predictors: (Constant), Tangibility					
b. Dependent Variable: Debt to Equity Ratio					

Source: Researcher 2017

According to table 4.34. ANOVA results show a P-Value of 0.000 which is in line with the fitted model at 0.000 helps us to conclude that our regression model results are significantly better prediction of company leverage (debt to Equity Ratio) rather than using the mean value of tangibility indicators (Fixed Assets/Total Assets)

Table 4.34. ANOVA: Company Tangibility and Debt to Equity Ratio

Model		Sum of Squares	df	Mean Square	F	Sig.
1	Regression	1.337	1	1.337	18.101	.000[b]
	Residual	19.643	266	0.074		
	Total	20,979	267			
a. Dependent Variable: Debt to Equity Ratio						
b. Predictors: (Constant) Tangibility						

Source: Researcher 2017

By analyzing the results of Model 2 below (Table 4.35) its show that tangibility has negative results (Beta=-0.252) with (sig=0.000) significance level means that fixed assets tangibility negatively impacts debt to equity ratio and this leads to the conclusion of rejecting the Null hypothesis (H1a) that there is positive relationship between tangibility and debt to equity ratio.

Table 4.35 Regression- Tangibility and Debt to Equity Ratio Multicolliearnity tests -Coefficients

Coefficients								
Model		Unstandardized Coefficients		Standardized Coefficients	t	Sig.	Collinearity Statistics	
		B	Std. Error	Beta			Tolerance	VIF
1	(Constant)	.618	.040		15.603	.000		
	Tangibility	-.273	.064	-.252	-4.255	.000	1.000	1.000
a. Dependent Variable: Debt to Equity Ratio								

Source: Researcher 2017

Regression Analysis: Company Tangibility and Debt Ratio

Table 4.36 below explain the results of the regression analysis that determines the relationship between fixed assets tangibility and leverage. The independent variable is tangibility (Fixed assets divided by total assets) and the dependent variable is debt ratio. The results below show (R^2) Value of 0.011 which means that 1% of the variation in debt to ratio is explained by tangibility. The autocorrelation tests, Durban Watson statistic (0.665) shows that there is lack of autocorrelation between the model errors.

$$DRATIO_{i,t} = ß0 + ß1\ (TANG_{i,t}) + e\ Model\ 6$$

Table 4:36 Variation of the Regression Model – Tangibility and Debt Ratio

Model	R	R Square	Adjusted R Square	Std. Error of the Estimate	Durbin-Watson
5	0.106a	0.011	0.008	2.451	0.665
a. Predictors: (Constant) Tangibility					
b. Dependent Variable: Debt Ratio					

Source: Researcher 2017

The table below shows. ANOVA results with P-Value of 0.083. This is the above fitted model at 0.000 hence it helps us to conclude that our regression model results are significantly better prediction of company leverage (debt Ratio) rather than using the mean value of Tangibility.

Table 4.37. ANOVA: Company Tangibility and Debt Ratio

Model		Sum of Squares	df	Mean Square	F	Sig.
6	Regression	18252	1	18.252	3.037	.083b
	Residual	1598.532	266	6.010		
	Total	1616.78	267			
	a. Dependent Variable: Debt Ratio					
	b. Predictors: (Constant) Tangibility					

Source: Researcher 2017

By analyzing the results of Model 2 below (Table 4.38) show tangibility having negative results (Beta= -.1009) with (sig=0.083) significance level means that tangibility negatively impacts debt ratio and this leads to the conclusion of rejecting the Null hypothesis (H1b) that there is positive relationship between tangibility and debt ratio; These results corresponds with the correlation analysis above and contradicts the prediction of the pecking order and trade off theory.

Table 4.38. Regression- Tangibility and Debt to Equity Ratio Multicolliearnity tests -Coefficients

Coefficients							
Model	Unstandardized Coefficients		Standardized Coefficients	t	Sig.	Collinearity Statistics	
	B	Std. Error	Beta			Tolerance	VIF
2 (Constant)	2.210	.357		6.182	.000		
Tangibility	-1.009	.579	-.106	-1.743	.083	1.000	1.000
a. Dependent Variable: Debt Ratio							

Source: Researcher 2017

4.6.3 Discussion on Research Findings

The findings of this study show a negative relationship between tangibility (measured by fixed assets tangibility) and leverage of Tanzanian companies confirms to the prediction of the pecking order theory and findings of the previous studies but contrary to the prediction of the trade- off theory. Pecking order theory predicted on negative relationship between tangibility and leverage. More assets reduce the information asymmetry level hence leading to cheaper equity (Harris and Ravis 1991). The study findings Cornell et al (1996), Pandey 2001, and De Angelo and Masulis (1980) confirm a negative relationship between tangibility and leverage ratio which is similar to our study findings. The study findings suggest that as Tanzanian companies' assets increased collateral values also increase which means that the capability to raise funds through debts increases as lenders have more confidence with such companies

However, this study is contrary to trade off theory prediction. Trade off theory predicts a positive relationship between company net fixed assets and its level of leverage. Companies with more fixed assets tend to use the assets as collateral hence easy to access more debts (Myers and Majluf 1984). The trade-off theory further suggests that with increased level of tangibility, companies trust and confidence by the lending institutions increases, hence easy for them to access debts from the lenders.

Our findings are suggesting that Tanzanian companies have borrowed so much to finance their business operations but not necessarily influenced by collateral assets (tangibility) but other factors might have influenced the level of borrowings such as interest rates and difficult conditions of companies to meet the listing conditions in the country. Findings by Frank and Goyal (2006) confirm these predictions as the study found a positive relationship between tangibility and leverage. Similar findings on positive relationship between tangibility and leverage are study by Shah and Khan (2007), Gaud et al (2003) who found a positive significant relationship between tangibility and leverage. These studies confirmed the prediction of the trade-off theory.

4.6.4 Conclusions

The study examined the relationship between tangibility (Fixed assets tangibility) and leverage of Tanzanian companies as predicted by pecking order theory and trade off theory. The study found that the Tangibility of listed companies was higher than that of the unlisted companies, though over the study period the tangibility indicators of boss companies was increasing a proportional rate. Therefore, further research is needed to study the causes of such major variation in fixed assets tangibility.

The study also found negative relationship between Tangibility and leverage which is contrary POT and TOT. This suggests that majority of Tanzanian had adequate fixed assets for collateralization and hence allowed these companies to use debts as the means of financing their business operations. These suggestions are also backed up with the existence of many unlisted companies that are not listed in the stock exchange which makes difficulty for these funds to raise funds through equity funds. The study did not establish the relationship between short term assets tangibility and leverage of Tanzanian companies. This suggest that further studies could be necessary to understand the relationship between short term assets tangibility and leverage. The study did not confirm on the relationship of tangibility with other capital structure theories hence a suggestion for further study.

The study also used only one measures of tangibility namely fixed assets tangibility in this particular study. The use of short term assets tangibility is likely to bring new findings. The use of only 59 companies also limits the conclusions of the findings. Conclusions drawn from this study may imply that if other indicators of tangibility and more companies could be used in further studies the results might reveal different findings which may concur on not concur with the predictions of the pecking order or trade off theories.

4.7. Research Findings: The Influence of Company Size and Company Leverage

This section presents the descriptive statistics on relationship between company size and leverage of both listed and unlisted companies, hypothesis testing, discussion of the research findings in relation to the consistency pecking order theory, static trade off theory prediction and findings of the previous studies and finally the conclusions and recommendations. The specific research question is re-stated here under *"To what extent does company size influence the leverage of Tanzanian companies as implied by trade off theory and pecking order theory?* The results are presented hereunder:

4.7.1. Summary Statistics

Table 4.39 below shows the characteristic of assets tangibility of both listed and unlisted companies for the period 2007 to 2014. Company size was measured by logarithm of net sales (Log of Sales). The results show that listed companies have higher mean (SD) scores of 23.59 (2.709) with minimum and maximum value of 12 and 27 respectively in 53 observations. Listed companies have mean (SD) core of 21.68 (4.421) with minimum and maximum value of 0 and 28 respectively in 204 observations. These results mean that listed companies net sales were higher than the net sales of unlisted companies.

Table 4.39: Descriptive statistics of Companies Tangibility

Variable	Listed Company	Unlisted Company
Mean	23.59	21.68
Standard Deviation	2.709	4.421
Minimum	12	0
Maximum	27	28
Observation	53	204

Source: Researcher 2017

Looking at the individual sector in totality companies revealed different performance characteristics in terms of net sales during the period of study. Results under table 4.40. below reveals that the sectors with higher mean (SD) in terms of size were agricultural sector with mean (SD) Scores of 26.40(0.387), Telecommunication 23.66(0.595) beverage companies 24.20(3.127), Aviation Services 24.10(0.638), Automobile 23.07(0.897), Media 22.52(1.806) and manufacturing 22.07(5.928) Tourism 22.84(2.025), Construction 21.38(2.971) and hospitality 21.38(2.971). Sectors with lower mean (SD) scores include the Air Transport 18.75(0.230), Printing 18.28 (1.843) and information technology 17.21 (0.114). The variation of sectors performances in sales is explained by factors not studied by this particular study.

Table 4.40: Descriptive statistics of Sector Size (Log of Sales)

Company Sector	Mean	Std. Deviation	Minimum	Maximum	N
Beverage	24.20	3.127	12	28	27
Telecommunication	23.66	.595	23	24	6
Tourism	22.84	2.025	20	25	13

Construction	21.77	1.419	19	24	50
Hospitality	21.38	2.971	16	25	28
Aviation Services	24.10	.638	24	25	6
Air Transport	18.75	.230	18	19	5
Manufacturing	22.07	5.928	0	27	78
Agriculture	26.40	.387	26	27	5
Automobile	23.07	.897	22	24	6
Printing	18.28	1.843	17	21	10
Media	22.52	1.806	17	24	12
IT	17.21	.114	17	17	4

Source: Researcher 2018

Trend Analysis of Companies Net sales

The following table (Table 4.41) and figure illustrates the trend analysis of company size of the listed and unlisted companies between year 2007 and 2014. The table below indicates listed companies had higher mean score (SD) of 21.93(5.88) as compared to 20.84(6.01) of that of unlisted companies. This means that listed companies have more sales as compared to unlisted companies. The results for 2008 show higher mean (SD) score of 23.81 (0.96) in size by listed companies against mean (SD) score of 0.21.71(4.41) of the unlisted companies. This shows that in 2008 the log of sales of listed companies increased by 7% compared to an increase 10% for unlisted company. The following year (2009) the results show higher mean (SD) score of 0.60 (0.124) in tangibility by listed companies against mean (SD) score of 0.54(0.289) of the unlisted companies. This shows that in 2008 the tangibility ratio of listed companies increased by 9% compared to an increase 4% for unlisted company. In year 2010 the results show higher mean (SD) scores of 23.97(2.38) in size by listed companies against mean (SD) score of 21.89(4.27) of the unlisted companies. This shows that in 2008 company size of listed companies increased by 0% compared to a decrease of 1% for unlisted company.

The following year (2011) listed companies had mean (SD) scores of 23.95(2.42) against mean score (SD)scores of 22.23(3.01) of unlisted companies. This shows that size of listed companies increased by 0 % and 2% decrease for unlisted companies. In year 2012 listed companies had mean (SD) scores of 23.76(3.54) against mean score (SD)scores of 21.94(3.43) of unlisted companies. This shows that size of listed companies decreased by 1 % and 1% decrease for unlisted companies. The following year (2013) listed companies had mean (SD) scores of 23.76(3.54) against mean score (SD)scores of 22.76(3.8) of unlisted companies. This shows that size of listed companies had no increase (0%) and increase of 4% for unlisted companies. The final year (2014) listed companies had mean (SD) scores of 21.09(3.28) against mean score (SD)scores of 24.25(3.13) of unlisted companies. This indicates a decrease of 11% for listed companies against an increase of 7% of size by the unlisted companies. The variation of company size is explained by the individual characteristic of the companies as well as well as unknown factors not investigated by this study

Table 4:41 Trend Analysis of Companies Net sales

	Listed Companies		Unlisted Companies	
Year	Mean (SD)	% Change	Mean (SD)	% Change
2007	21.93(5.88)		20.84(6.01)	
2008	23.81(0.96)	9%	21.71(4.41)	4%
2009	24.04(1.38)	1%	21.72(4.13)	0%
2010	23.97(2.38)	0%	21.89(4.27)	1%
2011	23.95(2.42)	0%	22.23(3.01)	2%
2012	23.76(3.54)	-1%	21.94(3.43)	-1%
2013	23.76(3.54)	0%	22.76(3.8)	4%
2014	21.09(3.28)	-11%	24.25(3.13)	7%

Source: Researcher 2018

Figure 4.7 below depicts the trend analysis of company size for both listed and unlisted companies for the period between year 2007 and 2007. The figure clearly depicts that the size of listed companies represented by the volume of sales was higher than the ones for unlisted companies throughout the years 2007 and 2013 and it started to drop thereafter till it went down below the volume of sales of the unlisted companies in 2014.

Figure 4.7: Trend Analysis of Company Size (2007-2014)

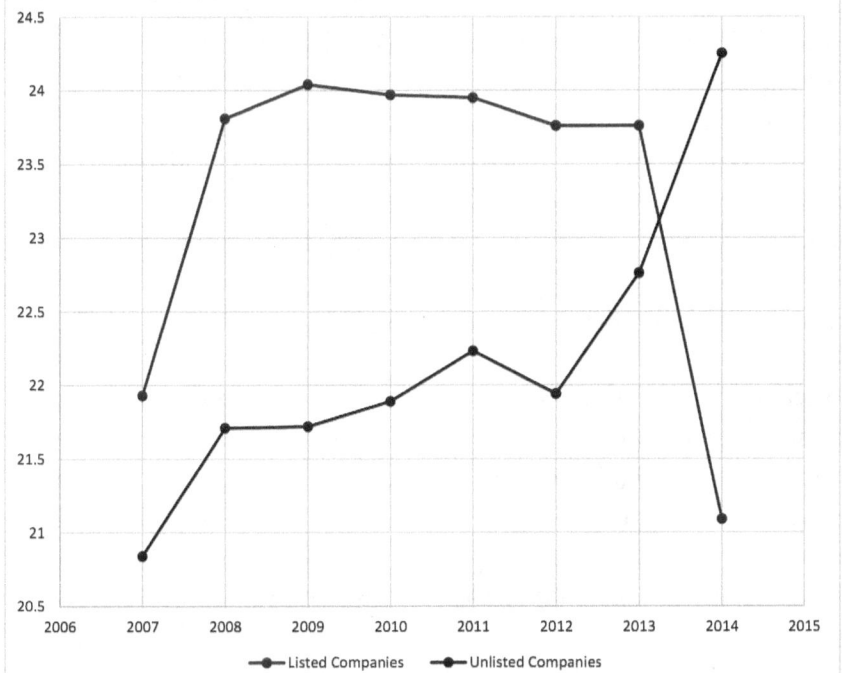

Source: Researcher 2018

4.7.2 Hypothesis testing

We test the relationship between tangibility and company leverage by using the Pearson correlation analysis and regression analysis. We re-state the hypothesis hereunder;

H5: There is a significant negative relationship between Company size and company leverage

Hypothesis five has another two minor hypotheses stated here under

H: 5a: There is a significant negative relationship between company size and debt to equity ratio
H: 5b: There is a significant negative relationship between company size and debt ratio

Correlation Analysis

Correlation analysis is performed (Table 4.42) to show the relationship between company size (measured by logarithm to sales) and leverage as dependent variable measured by debt ratio and debt to equity ratio. The results show that there is a significant negative correlation of -0.082 between company size and debt ratio to equity ratio. We therefore accept the minor Null hypothesis (H5a: *There is a significant negative relationship between company size and debt to equity ratio*) and conclude that there is negative correlation between company size and debt to equity ratio.

Correlation results also shows a negative relationship between company size and debt ratio (-0.090). We also accept the minor Null Hypothesis (H5b: There is a significant negative relationship between company size and leverage of Tanzanian Companies). We can therefore conclude that that there is negative relationship between company assets and leverage of Tanzanian companies (H5) as measured by debt ratio.

Table 4.42: Correlation Analysis – Company size and Leverage

	Logarithm of sales	Debt to Equity Ratio	Debt Ratio
Logarithm of Sales	1		
Debt to Equity Ratio	-.082**	1	
Debt Ratio	-.090	.658**	1

**. Correlation is significant at the 0.01 level (2-tailed).

Source: Researcher 2017

Regression Analysis: Company Tangibility and Debt to Equity Ratio

Table 4.43 below shows the regression results between company size and leverage of Tanzanian companies. The independent variable is company size and the dependent variable is leverage measured by debt to equity ratio. The table below shows (R^2) Value of 0.07 which means that only 7% of the variation in debt to equity ratio is explained by company size. Durban Watson statistic results (0.681) reveals no autocorrelation problem between the model errors

$$\text{D/ERATIO}_{i,t} = \beta 0 + \beta 1\ (\text{Log of Sales}_{i,t})) + e \qquad \text{Model 1}$$

Table 4:43 - Variation of the Regression Model – Company Size and Debt to Equity Ratio

Model	R	R Square	Adjusted R Square	Std. Error of the Estimate	Durbin-Watson
1	0.082ª	0.07	0.030	.276	0.0681

a. Predictors: (Constant), Company Size

b. Dependent Variable: Debt to Equity Ratio

Source: Researcher 2017

ANOVA results (Table 4.44) shows P-Value of 0.188 which is above the line with the fitted model at 0.000. This helps us to conclude that our regression model results are significantly better prediction of company leverage (debt to Equity Ratio) rather than using the mean value of log of sales indicators

Table 4.44. ANOVA: Company Size and Debt to Equity Ratio

Model		Sum of Squares	df	Mean Square	F	Sig.
1	Regression	0.333	1	0.133	1.745	.188ᵇ
	Residual	19.637	257	0.076		
	Total	19.771	258			
	a. Dependent Variable: Debt to Equity Ratio					
	b. Predictors: (Constant) Logarithm of Sales					

Source: Researcher 2017

By analyzing Model 2 results below (Table 4.45) it shows that log of sales which is the measure of company size has negative results (Beta=-0.005) with (sig=0.188) significance level means that log of sales (Company Size) negatively impacts debt to equity ratio and this leads to the conclusion of rejecting the Null hypothesis (H5a) that there is positive relationship between company size and debt to equity ratio.

Table 4.45 Regression- Company Size and Debt to Equity Ratio Multicolliearnity tests -Coefficients

Coefficients								
Model B		Unstandardized Coefficients		Standardized Coefficients	t	Sig.	Collinearity Statistics	
			Std. Error	Beta			Tolerance	VIF
1	(Constant)	.618	.040		15.603	.000		
	Log of Sales	-.005	.004	-.082	-1.321	.188	1.000	1.000
a. Dependent Variable: Debt to Equity Ratio								

Source: Researcher 2017

Regression Analysis: Company Profitability and Debt Ratio

Table 4.46 below explain the results of the regression analysis that determines the relationship between company size and leverage. The independent variable is log of sales and the dependent variable is debt ratio. The results below show (R^2) Value of 0.008 which means that only a small percentage (0.8%) of the debt to ratio is explained by company size (Log of Sales). The autocorrelation tests, Durban Watson statistic (0.658) shows that there is lack of autocorrelation between the model errors.

$$DRATIO_{i,t} = ß0 + ß1 (TANG_{i,t}) + e \qquad \text{Model 2}$$

Table 4:46 Variation of the Regression Model – Company Size and Debt Ratio

Model	R	R Square	Adjusted R Square	Std. Error of the Estimate	Durbin-Watson
1	0.090ª	0.008	0.004	2.482	0.658
a. Predictors: (Constant) Log of Sales					
b. Dependent Variable: Debt Ratio					

Source: Researcher 2017

The table below (Table 4.47 shows ANOVA results with P-Value of 0.147. This is the above fitted model at 0.000 hence it helps us to conclude that our regression model results are significantly better prediction of company leverage (debt Ratio) rather than using the mean value of log of sales (Company size).

Table 4.47 ANOVA: Company size and Debt Ratio

Model		Sum of Squares	df	Mean Square	F	Sig.
2	Regression	13.052	1	13052	2.119	.147[b]
	Residual	1583.265	257	6.161		
	Total	1596.317	258			
	a. Dependent Variable: Debt Ratio					
	b. Predictors: (Constant) Logarithm of Sales					

Source: Researcher 2017

By analyzing the results of Model 2 below (Table 4.48) it shows that log of sales which represents company size having negative results (Beta= -.054) with (sig=0.147) significance level means that company size negatively impacts debt ratio and this leads to the conclusion of rejecting the Null hypothesis (H1b) that there is positive relationship between company size and debt ratio; These results corresponds with the correlation analysis above and contradicts the prediction of the tradeoff theory but consistency to the postulates stated by the other theory (pecking order).

Table 4.48. Regression- Company Size and Debt Ratio Multicolliearnity tests -Coefficients

Coefficients								
Model		Unstandardized Coefficients		Standardized Coefficients	t	Sig.	Collinearity Statistics	
		B	Std. Error	Beta			Tolerance	VIF
2	(Constant)	2.883	.357		3.472	.001		
	Logarithm of Sales	-.054	.037	-0.090	-1.456	.147	1.000	1.000
a. Dependent Variable: Debt Ratio								

Source: Researcher 2017

4.7.3. Discussion to the Research Findings

The study results give evidence that there is existence of negative correlation between the research variables. Company size (logarithm of sales) is negatively correlated to debt to equity ratio as well as to debt ratio. This leads to conclude that there is negative relationship between company size and leverage of Tanzanian companies hence accepting the Null hypothesis (H5). The findings of this study suggest that company size increases the ability these companies will tend to use less more of its retained earnings to fund the business operations. Higher level of sales level is likely to increase the company profitability and hence the retained earnings. The findings of this study contradict to the prediction of the tradeoff theory and the prediction of the pecking order theory. Both theories predict for positive relationship between company size and leverage.

The findings of this study are also similar to few previous studies in other countries which confirmed our findings. Strebulaer and Yang (2006) study reveal a negative correlation between leverage and size. Ramalho and Vidigal da Silva (2009), studies found that company size was negatively related to the proportion of debts in capital structure of Portuguese companies. These results have implied that majority of Tanzanian companies are still small and remain unlisted in stock exchange for many years and they are likely to be borrowing more than the larger companies.

In terms of company sectors the agricultural, Telecommunication beverage Aviation Services Automobile Media and manufacturing, Tourism, Construction and hospitality sectors indicated higher mean (SD) scores meaning that majority of large companies were from these sectors. Sectors which indicated lower mean (SD) score includes the Air Transport, printing and information technology. These scores indicate that the companies operating in these sectors were small companies.

4.7.4. Conclusions

The study examined the relationship between company size (Log of Sales) and leverage of Tanzanian companies as predicted by pecking order theory and trade off theory. This study findings suggest that Pecking order theory (POT) and Trade off Theory (TOT) relevance cannot fully supported in Tanzanian companies as the findings did indicate that company size and leverage were negatively associated. The study found that size of listed companies was higher than that of the unlisted companies. This suggests that the size of majority Tanzanian unlisted companies is still small as compared to the listed companies. Therefore, further research is needed to study the causes of such major differences among Tanzanian companies.

The study also used only one measures of company size namely log of Sales in this particular study. The use of other measures (Total Assets) to measure company size might give different results. The study also used only two indicators of leverage while there are other types of indicators of leverage. The use of different indictors of leverage is likely to give different results hence a need for further research which might give different conclusions.

The use of only 59 companies to establish the relationship between size and leverage also limits the conclusions of the findings. Conclusions drawn from this study may imply that if other indicators of more companies could be used in further studies the results might reveal different findings which may concur to the predictions of the pecking order and trade off theories.

CHAPTER FIVE

SUMMARY, CONCLUSIONS AND RECOMMENDATIONS

5.1 Introduction

Capital structure studies has been undertaken by different scholars across the globe but studies on developed countries has been leading as compared to less developed countries like Tanzania. At the same time, we noted that many studies have been on listed companies and few on unlisted companies. Few studies devoted to capital structure of both listed and unlisted companies. In Tanzania only, few studies on capital structure were on listed companies. This study therefore concentrated to the study the of both listed and unlisted companies for the period between 2007 and 2014.

5.2 Summary of the thesis

The study intended to assess the capital structure determinants of listed and unlisted manufacturing firms in Tanzania. The specifically the study examined the influence of company specific factors (liquidity, profitability, tangibility and size) on leverage of Tanzanian companies.

Chapter 1 – This chapter gives the background information on capital structure studies and explains the research objectives of the study. The main research objective was to assess the capital structure determinants factors of listed and unlisted companies in Tanzania. Specific objectives of the study (1) To establish the degree of leverage among listed and unlisted companies in Tanzania

(2) To examine the extent to which liquidity influences the leverage of Tanzanian Companies as implied by the pecking order theory and Trade off Theory (3) To explore the extent to which profitability affects the leverage of Tanzanian Companies suggested by the pecking order and trade-off theory (4) As implied by pecking order and trade-off theory, examine the extent to which tangibility influences the leverage of Tanzanian Companies. (5) To establish the extent to which company size influences leverage of Tanzanian Companies as suggested trade off theory and pecking order theory

Chapter 2- Explains the literature review of the study. This chapter has discussed the underlying epistemology of the capital structures and theories that have been developed by different scholars over the years. Further discussions have been on determinants factors of capital structures and their influence on leverage of both listed and unlisted companies across the globes. Majority of capital structure studies has been on listed companies rather than the unlisted companies in developed world and not in the underdeveloped countries such as Tanzania. The chapter also gives empirical evidences of capital structure determinants and their relationship to company leverage as measured by debt to equity ratio and debt ratio.

Chapter 3 Discusses the research methodology and conceptual framework. The conceptual frameworks (Fig 3.1) firstly one discusses how capital structure determinants factors (Tangibility, Liquidity, Profitability and company Size) as independent variables relate to company leverage (Dependent variable). Debt to equity ratio and debt ratio are the measures of leverage for this particular study. Further, the chapter discusses the methods used to collect the data. Panel data is collected of both listed and unlisted companies is collected from the financial statements for the period starting 2007 to 2014 and excluding all data from all financial services companies.

Chapter 4- This chapter explains the findings of each research objective and research questions. The summary of findings for each research objective is explained hereunder

Research objective 1

The first research aimed at underscoring the degree of leverage among listed and unlisted companies in Tanzania. Research findings reveal that as far as debt to equity ratio is concerned, listed companies had on average of higher mean scores (Median) of 0.465 [0.397] as compared to mean scores (Median) of unlisted companies 0.467[0.420] by which means debts of listed companies represents 46% of total equity as compared to 47% of the unlisted companies. The results suggest that all companies have almost the same dependence on debts on financing their business operations despite the fact that listed companies have options of using more equity to finance their business operations. As far as debt ratio is concerned listed companies have higher mean (median) scores of 1.660[0.618] as compared to lower mean (median) scores of 1.651[0.716]. This suggests that are listed companies having more assets to cover the outstanding liabilities than their counterparty.

Research objective 2

The second objective of the study aimed at investigating the influence of company liquidity on leverage among Tanzanian listed and unlisted companies. Panel data of 59 companies for the period 2007 -2014 were obtained from the financial statements and used for the study. We tested if company liquidity measured by current ratio was related to leverage ratios. Company leverage was measured by debt ratio as well as the debt to equity ratio. The study findings show that company liquidity was negatively related to both debt to equity and debt ratios. These findings therefore lead to the rejection of the hypothesis and conclude that negative relationship exists between liquidity and leverage. Our findings are similar with few previous studies and consistent to the pecking order predictions but not in conformance to the of postulates of the postulates of the Tradeoff Theory

Research Objective 3

The third objective of the study aimed in examining the influence of company profitability on company leverage. The study objective considered the independent variable to be as profitability as the measured by Return on Assets (ROA) and Return on equity (ROE)and company leverage measured by debt ratio and debt to equity ratio as the dependent variable. Panel data were collected from financial statements of both listed and unlisted companies totaling to 59 companies for the period between 2007 and 2014. We test the hypothesis by use of correlation and regression analysis to see whether a positive relationship exists between profitability and company leverage.

The Findings reveal that return on assets (ROA) was positively correlated to both debt ratio and debt to equity ratio. Further findings reveal that Return on Equity (ROE)and leverage ratios were also positively related. Our Findings confirms the previous studies findings though contrary to pecking order but consistent to the predictions of Trade of theory.

Research Objective 4

The fourth objective of the study aimed in examining the relationship between Asset Tangibility and Leverage of Tanzanian Companies. The study adopted company tangibility as the independent variable measured by fixed assets tangibility and the dependent variable as company leverage measured by debt ratio and debt to equity ratio. Panel data were collected from financial statements of both listed and unlisted companies total to 59 companies for the period between 2007 and 2014. Correlation and regression analysis were used to test if tangibility was related to company leverage. Study findings indicate that asset tangibility and leverage was negatively correlated. This is evidenced by negative correlations between tangibility and debt ratio as well as the debt to equity ratio.

Further findings reveal. Our Findings are consistent with the findings of the previous studies but not consistent to pecking order theory trade off Theory predictions.

Research Objective 5

The fifth objective of the study intended to examine if size of the Tanzanian companies do have influence on their leverage. The study adopted company size (Log of Sales) as the independent variable measured and the dependent variable as company leverage measured by debt ratio and debt to equity ratio. Panel data were collected from financial statements of both listed and unlisted companies totaling to 59 companies for the period between 2007 and 2014. Correlation and regression analysis were used to test for existence of positive relationship between these two variables (size as independent variable and leverage as a dependent variable) as per hypothesis five (H5). The Findings reveal that company size and debt to equity ratio are negatively correlated but there is a negative relationship between company size and debt ratio. Further findings reveal. Our Findings are consistent not with the findings of the previous studies and not consistent to pecking order theory and trade off Theory predictions. We therefore rejected the Null Hypothesis (H5).

5.3 Significance of the study

This study has not developed any new capital structure theory. However, it has contributed to the body of knowledge that Pecking order assumptions and trade off theory postulates are relevant and valid in Tanzania business environment. It also shows that the studied company specific factors namely profitability, tangibility, size and liquidity have significant impact to the leverage of Tanzanian companies as well. This study contributes to the body of knowledge by giving profound insights to scholars, academicians, and practitioners to understand that the capital structure determinants that influence leverage in developed countries have impact on leverage in context of Tanzanian companies apart from the available literature for similar studies from many developed countries based mainly on listed companies and few unlisted companies.

5.4 Limitation of the Study

The secrecy nature of unlisted companies in Tanzania which majority of them were private companies posed a limitation of getting more unlisted companies to be part study. A sample of fifty-nine companies may be considered as small as compared to more companies operating in Tanzania. Majority of the companies were also concentrated in major cities of the country leaving companies in small cities.

5.5. Conclusions and Recommendations

This study aimed at examining the degree of leverage among Tanzanian companies and to establish the relationship between company liquidity, profitability, tangibility, size, age and leverage of Tanzanian companies relevant to the predominance capital structure theories developed over time which include the Pecking order, Trade off theory and organizational life cycle theory.

Conclusions on Degree of Leverage

The study findings on the first specific objective of the study reveal that Tanzanian companies leverage among listed and unlisted companies are significantly different. Unlisted companies have revealed higher debt ratios and debt to equity ratio as indicator of leverage levels as compared to listed companies. This means that in Tanzania, unlisted companies use more debts to finance their business operations as compared to the listed ones and these companies have less access to equity funding available through stock listing at the Dar-es-salaam stock exchange.

Conclusions on liquidity influence on Companies Leverage.

The study findings reveal for a negative correlation between company liquidity and company leverage as measured by debt ratio and debt to equity ratio. These findings show the validity, applicability and relevance of the pecking order theory in Tanzania. The postulates of the trade-off theory as far as liquidity is concerned are not valid. This means that companies in Tanzania especially those with high liquidity do not borrow much from financial institutions, they use their cashflow to finance their business operations instead of debt option. This suggest that the borrowing conditions are not favorable and cost of borrowing in Tanzania is high. It is recommended from this study that government policy makers especially those making decisions affecting the lending institutions should consider re-examining the borrowing conditions as well reduce the interest rates to encourage companies to borrow money from these financial institutions. In order to maintain adequate liquidity of the companies, corporate managers of Tanzanian companies should therefore continue making decisions that do have positive influence on the liquidity of their companies. This will help their companies to have enough cash flow to finance their business operations without relying on debts as lower liquidity can cause companies to opt to use more debts to finance their activities

Conclusions on profitability and Company leverage

The study found that the profitability of unlisted companies was higher than that of the listed companies and over the study period the profitability indicators (ROA and ROE) of listed companies was declining at higher rate than the ones of the unlisted companies. The study also found that despite of the higher profitability of the unlisted companies, these companies still opted to use debts and not much of their retained earnings to finance their business operations. These findings are backed up with the existence of few companies that are listed in the stock exchange that are able to raise funds through equity funds. It is recommended that the government should revise its financial and economic policies in order to encourage profitable companies to list in stock exchange in order to access equity funding.

Conclusions on tangibility and leverage

The study found that the Tangibility of listed companies was higher than that of the unlisted companies, though over the study period the tangibility indicators of boss companies was increasing a proportional rate. Therefore, further research is needed to study the causes of such major variation in fixed assets tangibility. The study also found negative relationship between Tangibility and leverage which is contrary POT and TOT. This suggests that majority of Tanzanian companies had adequate fixed assets for collateralization and hence allowed these companies to use debts as the means of financing their business operations. These suggestions are also backed up with the existence of many unlisted companies that are not listed in the stock exchange which makes difficulty for these funds to raise funds through equity funds

Conclusions on size and leverage

The study examined the relationship between company size (Log of Sales) and leverage of Tanzanian companies as predicted by the trade-off and pecking order theories. This study findings suggest that Pecking order theory (POT) and Trade off Theory (TOT) relevance cannot fully supported in Tanzanian companies as the findings have revealed a negative relationship between company size and leverage. The study found that size of listed companies was higher than that of the unlisted companies. This suggests that the size of majority Tanzanian unlisted companies is still small as compared to the listed companies. Therefore, further research is needed to study the causes of such major variation between the listed and unlisted companies.

Overall Conclusion

The overall conclusion of this study shows that unlisted companies in Tanzania are more leveraged than the listed ones **and** that there are mixed types of relationship between firm characteristics and leverage of Tanzanian companies. These types of relationships either confirms or contradicts the predictions of both the tradeoff theory and pecking order theory. The findings reveal positive relationship between liquidity and leverage confirming the pecking order but contravening the tradeoff theory. On profitability, the results show that unlisted companies are more profitable and there is a positive relationship between profitability and leverage which is in conformity to the tradeoff theory but contrary to pecking order theory. However, findings on tangibility findings indicate a negative relationship to leverage which is in accordance to pecking order but against the postulates of the Tradeoff theory. As far as company size is concerned the study suggest for existence of negative correlation between the study variables.

5.6. Further Research direction

Research degree on Degree of Leverage

The study finding reveal that both companies in Tanzania use debts to finance their business activities, though unlisted companies use more debts than their counterparty. Listing conditions can be eased to help unlisted companies access equity funding, same way as listed companies.

Further research study is needed to investigate what kind of policies or strategies are needed in Tanzania to encourage more companies to access funding through equity.

Research direction on Liquidity and Leverage

The study used only one variable to measure liquidity (Current ratio against two variables of dependent variable (debt ratio and debt equity ratio). There is numerous measures for liquidity and leverage. Therefore, conducting a further research based on use of more variables indicators of liquidity and leverage could result into different findings and conclusions. The study was also limited in terms of sample characteristics as few companies participated in the study due to difficulties of obtaining financial statements from the private companies. The secrecy nature of private companies leads to difficulties of more companies participating in the study. Given the fact that one is able to increase the sample of private unlisted companies to participate in the study, the likely results might indicate a different relationship between company liquidity and leverage

Research direction on Profitability on Leverage

The study did not establish the reasons for the decline in return on assets and return on equity. Further research on what really influences profitability of Tanzania companies over time is needed in order to establish the causes of such major declines and develop strategies to enhance the company profitability. Further research study is needed to investigate what kind of Policies or strategies are needed in Tanzania to encourage more companies to access funding through equity.

Research direction on Tangibility and Leverage

The study did not establish the relationship between short term assets tangibility and leverage of Tanzanian companies. This suggest that further studies could be necessary to understand the relationship between short term assets tangibility and leverage. The study did not confirm on the relationship of tangibility with other capital structure theories hence a suggestion for further study. The study also used only one measures of tangibility namely fixed assets tangibility in this particular study. The use of short term assets tangibility is likely to bring new findings. The use of only 59 companies also limits the conclusions of the findings. Conclusions drawn from this study may imply that if other indicators of tangibility and larger sample of companies could be used in further studies the results might reveal different findings which may concur on not concur with the trade- off theory or the pecking order assumptions.

Research direction on Size and Leverage

The study used only one measures of company size namely log of Sales in this particular study. The use of other measures (Total Assets) to measure company size might give different results. The study also used only two indicators of leverage while there are other types of indicators of leverage. The use of different indictors of company size is likely to give different results hence a need for further research which might give different conclusions. Conclusions drawn from this study may imply that if other indicators of more companies could be used in further studies the results might reveal different findings which may concur to the predictions of the pecking order and trade off theories.

Overall future research direction

Apart from the above recommendations on further research on individual capital structure determinants, further research can be carried on to understand the influence of other capital structure determinants on leverage of Tanzanian companies. Previous empirical evidences show that more company characteristics, country specific factors can influence the leverage of companies. Since our study was limited to only four determinant factors namely liquidity, tangibility, profitability and size, the recommendation is made for further research on other capital structure determinants.

REFERENCES

Ahmad, N and Aris, Y (2015). Does Age of the Firm Determine Capital Structure Decision? Evidence from Malaysian Trading and Service Sector. *International Business Management, 9(3), 200-207*

Akinlo, O. (2011). Determinants of capital structure: Evidence from Nigerian panel data. *African Economic and Business Review, 9(1), 1-16*

Antoniou, A, Guney Y and Paudyal, K *(2007)* "Determinants of Corporate Capital Structure: Capital Market Oriented versus Bank Oriented Institutions," *Journal of Financial and Quantitative Analysis*

Akhtar S (2005). The Determinants of Capital Structure for Australian Multinational and Domestic Corporations, Australian *Journal of Management, Vol.30, No.2, 321-341, 2005*

Affandi, S., Wan M. and Abdul S (2012). Capital Structure of Property Companies in Malaysia Based on Three Capital Structure Theories. *South East Asian Journal of Contemporary Business, Economics and Law*, [e-journal] 1.

Akhtar, S., & Oliver, B. (2009). Determinants of capital structure for Japanese multinational and domestic corporations. *International Review of Finance, No 9*(1–2), 1–26.

Ali, L. (2011). The determinants of leverage of the listed-textile companies in India. *European Journal of Business and Management, 3*(12), 54–59.

Antoniou, A., Guney, Y., & Paudyal, K. (2002). The determinants of corporate capital structure: Evidence from European countries. *Department of Economics and Finance, University of Durham.*

Ahmed, M, Adesina O, Babatunde (2016) Empirical evidence on capital structure determinants in NIGERIA Journal of Economics and International Finance Vol. 8(6), pp.

Alexis K, Bagher A Milad S Determinants of Capital Structure and Speed of Adjustment: Evidence from Iran and Australia. *International Journal of Business Administration Vol. 9, No. 1; 2018*

Booth, L., Aivazian, V., Demirguc-Kunt, A. and Maksimovic, V. (2001), "Capital structures in developing countries", *The Journal of Finance, Vol. LVI No. 1, pp. 87-130*

Brigham, E. F. & Ehrhardt, M. C. (2004). *Financial Management: Theory and Practice,* 11th Edition, South-Western College Publishers, New York.

Brigham, E Eugene F and Joel F. (2004). *Fundamentals of Financial Management.* Forth Edition, USA, South Western Thomson Learning.

Bayeh K (2013) Impact of Firm Level Factors on Capital Structure: Evidence from Ethiopian Insurance Companies. *Global Journal of Management and Business Research Finance Volume 13 Issue 4*

Cassar, G., Holmes, S. (2003), "Capital structure and financing of SMEs: Australian evidence". *Journal of Accounting and Finance, Vol. 43 No.2, pp. 123–47.*

Campello, M. Giambina E. (2011), "Capital structure and the redeploy ability of tangible assets", *Tinbergen Institute Discussion Paper, No.11-091/2/DSF24.*

Cekrezi, A. (2015) 'Internal factors which influence capital structure choice of Albanian firms', *Research Journal of Finance and Accounting, Vol. 6, No. 8, pp.168–175.*

Shrabanti P2014). A Study on Capital Structure determinants of Indian Steel companies. *Global Business and Management Research: An International Journal* 4(4):89-98.

Damodaran A (2001). Corporate Finance; Theory and Practice. New York: John Wiley and Sons

De Jong, A., Kabir, R. and Nguyen, T.T. (2008), "Capital structure around the world: The roles of firm- and country – specific determinants", *Journal of Banking and Finance*, Vol. 32, pp. 1954-196

Diamond, D (1989, Monitoring and reputation: the choice between bank loans and directly placed debt, *Journal of Political Economy 99, 689-721*.

Donaldson G (1961), Corporate Debt Capacity. A Study of Corporate Debt Policy Determination of Corporate Debt Capacity, *Boston Division of Research, Harvard School of Business Administration*

Daskalakis, N., Psillaki, M. (2008), "Do country of firm explain capital structure? Evidence from SMEs in France and Greece", *Applied financial economics, Vol. 18, No. 2, pp. 87-97*.

Daskalakis, N., Thanou, E. (2010), "Capital structure of SMEs: to what extent does size matter?", *Available at: http://papers.ssrn.com/sol3/papers. cfm?abstract_id=1683161 (Accessed on: April 18, 2017*

Deari, F., Deari, M. (2009), "The determinants of capital structure: evidence from Macedonian listed and unlisted companies (not complete)

Degryse, H., Goeij, P., Kappert, P. (2010), "The impact of firm and industry characteristics on small firm's capital structure", *Small Bus Econ, Vol. 38, No. 4, pp. 431-447*.

Drobetz, W., and R. Fix. 2003. 'What are the Determinants of the Capital Structure? Some Evidence for Switzerland.' *Working Paper 4/03, University of Basel*

Degryse, H., Goeij, P., Kappert, P. (2010), "The impact of firm and industry characteristics on small firm's capital structure", *Small Bus Econ, Vol. 38, No. 4, pp. 431-447.*

D. Forte, L. A. Barros, W. T. Nakamura (2013) Determinants of the Capital Structure of Small and Medium Sized Brazilian Enterprises *Brazilian Administration Review, Vol. 10(3), pp. 347-369,*

Dharmendra Singh (2016) A Panel Data Analysis of Capital Structure Determinants: An Empirical Study of Non-Financial Firms in Oman International. *Journal of Economics and Financial Issues, 2016, 6(4), 1650-1656.*

Dejan M, Ksenija Denčić-M, Ema L (2013) The Determinants of Capital Structure in Emerging Capital Markets: Evidence from Serbia European *Research Studies, pp. 98-119 Vol. XVI*

Elliot, B and Elliot, J (2002): Financial Accounting and Reporting. 12th Edition, London, Prentice Hall *European Journal of Economics, Finance and Administrative Sciences, Vol 10, pp 233-243*

Ellili N. and Farouk S (2011). Examining the Capital Structure Determinants: Empirical Analysis of Companies Traded on Abu Dhabi Stock Exchange, *International Research Journal of Finance and Economics, No.67, 82-96, 2011.*

Esperança, J.P., P.M.G. Ana and A.G. Mohamed. 2003. "Corporate debt policy of small firms: An empirical (re)examination". *Journal of Small Business and Enterprise Development, Vol 10(1): 62–80*

Emilio Colombo (2010) Determinants of corporate capital structure: evidence from Hungarian firms, *Applied Economics, 33:13, 1689-1701*

Frank M Goyal V (2003). Capital Structure Decisions, *AFA San Diego Meetings 2003,* http://ssrn.com

Fama, E and French, K (1988). R., 1988, "Testing trade – off and pecking order predictions about dividends and debt", *The Review of Financial Studies, No 15, 1-33*

Farimah R, Forough R, Mohamed A and Jamshid S (2010). The Effect of Capital Structure on the Profitability of Pharmaceutical Companies The Case of Iran. *Iran Journal of Pharmaceutical Research. 12(3): 573*

Fernanda M and Leonor S, Carlos Miguel A (2018) Capital structure of Portuguese hotel firms: a structural equation modelling approach. *Tourism & Management Studies, 14(SI1), 2018, 73-82.*

Ghasema and Ab Razak (2016). The impact of liquidity on Capital Structure: Evidence from Malaysia: *International Journal of Economics and Finance. Vol 8 No 10, 2016, 130-139*

Graham & Harvey C (2001). The theory and Practice of corporate Finance; Evidence from the field, *Journal of Financial economics, 60, 187-243*

Gaud, P, Jani E, Hoesli M and Bender A (2005) "The Capital Structure of Swiss Companies: *An empirical analysis using dynamic panel Data,*" *European Financial Management, vol. 11, p. 51-69.*

Ghazouani, T. (2013), The Capital Structure through the Trade-Off Theory: Evidence from Tunisian Firm, *International Journal of Economics and Financial Issues, 3(3), 625-636.*

Frank, M.Z., and V.K. Goyal (2009) "Capital structure Decisions: Which factors are reliably important?" *Financial Management, vol. 38, p. 1-37*

Gajural, D.P. (2005) "Capital structure Management in Nepalese Enterprises," *Corporate Finance Journals, Working paper series.*

Harris, M., Raviv, A. (1991) "The theory of capital structure", *Journal of Finance, Vol. 46, No. 1, pp. 297-355.*

Herciu, M., Ogrean, C., Belascu, L. (2012), "Leveraging tangible and intangible assets by using a possible firm competitiveness index", *Global business and economics review, Vol. 14, No. 1/2, pp. 115-124.*

Hall T.W (2012). The collateral channel: Evidence on leverage and asset tangibility, *Journal of Corporate Finance, Vol.18, No.3, 570-583, 2012.*

Hasby Hamyat, Buyung Sarita, Hasbudin, Sujono (2017)4: The Effect of Firm size and Diversification on Capital Structure and Firm Value (Study in Manufacturing Sector in Indonesia Stock Exchange). *The International Journal of Engineering and Science Volume 6 (6), 50-61*

Harc M (2014): The relationship between tangible assets and capital structure of small and medium-sized companies in Croatia. *XXVIII, BR. 1/2015. str. 213-224*

Hall, G.C., P.J. Hutchinson and N. Michaela's. 2004. "Determinants of the capital structures of European SMEs". *Journal of Business Finance and Accounting, 31(5/6): 711–28*

Hamid A, Bashir A. and Muhammad Z (2013) The Co-determinants of Capital Structure and Stock Returns: Evidence from the Karachi Stock Exchange, *The Lahore Journal of Economics 18; 1 (Summer 2013): pp. 81–92*

Ishaya C, Sannomo G and Abu O (2013): Determinants of Capital Structure in the Nigerian Chemical and Paint Sector: International Journal of Humanities and Social Science "Vol 3 No 15, 247-263

Jahanzeb, A., Bajuri, N. H., Karami, M., & Ahmadimousaabad, A. (2014). Trade-Off Theory, Pecking Order Theory and Market Timing Theory: A Comprehensive Review of Capital

Jensen, M and Meckling, W (1976): "Theory of the firm: managerial behavior, agency costs and capital structure." Journal of Financial Economics,3, pp 11- 25

Jacinta CMahfuzur and Selvam S (2017) The determinants of capital structure: Evidence from public listed companies in Malaysia, Singapore and Thailand.

Kim W.S & Soverson, E.H (1986). Evidence on the impact of the Agency costs of Debt on Corporate Debt Policy.' *Journal of Financial and Quantitative Analysis, Vol 16 p 131-144*

Koksal, B., Orman, C., Oduncu, A. (2013), "Determinants of capital structure: evidence from a major emerging market economy

La Rocca, M., La Rocca, T., Cariola, A. (2009), "Small business financing. Financial preferences throughout the life cycle of a firm",

Leary, M. T., & Roberts, M. R. (2010). The pecking order, debt capacity, and information asymmetry. *Journal of Financial Economics, 95*(3), 332–355.

Lemmon, M. L., Roberts, Mand Zender, J. F. (2008). Back to the beginning: Persistence and the cross-section of corporate capital structure. *The Journal of Finance, 63*(4), 1575–1608.

Machogu M. and Bundala M. (2012). Do Tanzanian Companies practice pecking order theory, agency costs theory or trade off Theory? An Empirical study in Tanzanian Listed Companies. *International Journal of Economics and Financial Issues, Vol 2, No 4, 2012, pp 401-422*

Myers, S. (1984) The capital structure puzzle, *Journal of Finance, 39,* 575-592.

Myers, S.C. (2001), "Capital structure", *The Journal of Economic Perspectives, Vol. 15No. 2, pp. 81-102*

Myers, Stewart C.and Nicholas S. Majluf,(1984), corporate financing and investment decisions when firms have information those investors do not have, *Journal of Financial Economics Vol 13, 187-221*

Mahmoud, W., & Zakaria, R. (2007). Profitability and capital structure of the property and construction sectors in Malaysia. *Pacific Rim Property Research Journal, 13(1), 92-105*

Majluf M (1984), Corporate Financing and Investment Decisions when Firms have information investors do not have *Journal of Financial Economics No 2*

Michaelas, N., Chittenden, F. and Poutziouris, P.(1999), Financial Policy and Capital Structure Choice in U.K. SMEs: Empirical Evidence from Company Panel Data, *Small Business Economics, Vol12: pp113 – 130*

Md-Yusuf, M., Mohamad Yunus, F. and Md Supaat, N (2013) 2013. Determinants of Capital Structure in Malaysia Electrical and Electronic Sector. *World Academy of Science, Engineering and Technology, [e-journal]78Available at: www.waset.org/journals/waset/v78/v78-156.pdf* [Accessed 10 April 2018]

Modigliani, F., & Miller, M. H. (1963). Corporate income taxes and the cost of capital: A correction. *The American Economic Review*, 433–443.

Mouna A, Ye Jianmu and Kenza B (2018) Firm's Capital Structure Determinants and Financing Choice by Industry in Morocco. *International Journal of Management Science and Business Administration Volume 4, Issue 3, Pages 41-51*

Masoud, N. (2014) 'The determinants of capital structure choice: evidence from Libyan firms', *Research Journal of Finance and Accounting, Vol. 5, No. 1, pp.67–83*

Thippayana, P. (2014) 'Determinants of capital structure in Thailand', *Procedia – Social and Behavioral Sciences, Vol. 143, pp.1074–1077.*

Mishra, C., 2011. Determinants of Capital Structure – A Study of Manufacturing Sector PSUs in India. *International Conference on Financial Management and Economics IPEDR, [e-journal] Available at: www.ipedr.com/vol11/48-W00033.pdf [Accessed 18 May 2018].*

Michael C, Stevie S (2012). The determinants of corporate Capital Structure: Evidence from Japanese Companies Journal *of International Business Research, Volume 11, Special Issue, Number 3, 2012 pp121-13*

Mawih, K., Maha S (2015) THE Determinants of capital structure: AN empirical study of Omani listed industrial companies. *Business: Theory and Practice Vol16(2): 159–167*

Nishat, M., and W. Allah (2008) "Capital structure choice in an Emerging Market: *Evidence from Listed firms In Pakistan," 21st Australian finance and Banking Conference 2008 paper.*

Nelson V, António, C and Elísio B (2015). The Determinants of the Capital Structure of Listed on Stock Market Non-Financial Firms: Evidence for Portugal. *FEP Working Paper no 555, page 1-41*

Nguyen T, Nguyen P, Dang T andThu Hang (2017). The Determinants of Capital Structure for Vietnamese Real Estate Listed Companies *International Journal of Economics and Financial Issues, 2017, 7(4), 270-28*

Ozkan A (2001) Determinants of capital structure and Adjustment to long run target. Evidence from UK Company panel data. *Journal of Business Finance and Accounting, Vol 28 (1-2) 175-198*

Onaolapo, A & Kajola S, (2010) Capital Structure and Firm Performance: Evidence from Nigeria *European Journal of Economics, 25,1450-1460*

Ozkan A.(2001), "Determinants of capital structure and adjustment to long-run target: evidence from UK company panel data", *Journal of Business Finance & Accounting 28, 175-198.*

Pinkova P (2002)Determinants of capital structure: evidence from the Czech automotive industry. *Acta univ. agric. et silvic. Mendel. Brun., 2012, LX, No. 7, pp. 217–224*

Qi, M. and La, B.(2010). Firm Characteristics as Determinants of Capital Structures in Australia. Int. J. of the Economics of Business, [e-journal]17 (3). Available through: (http://libweb.anglia.ac.uk Accessed 18 May 2018)

Rajan, R.G. and L. Zingales(1995). "What do we know about capital structure: Some evidence from international data". *Journal of Finance*, 50: 1421–60

Ross, S. (1977). 'The Determination of Financial Structure: The Incentive Signaling Approach.' Bell Journal of Economics 8 (1): 23–40

Ramalho, J. J. S., & Vidigal da Silva, J. (2009), A Two-Part Fractional Regression Model for the Financial Leverage Decisions of Micro, Small, Medium and Large Firms', *Quantitative Finance, vol. 9, no. 5, pp. 621-636*

Rafiu O.S, Obafemi A (2009). The effect of Capital structure on profitability. An empirical Analysis of listed firms in Nigeria. T*he International Journal of Business and Finance Research, Vol 3(2)*

Sibilkov, V. (2009). Asset liquidity and capital structure. *Journal of Financial and Quantitative Analysis, 44*(05), 1173-

Šarlija, N., & Harc, M. (2012). The impact of liquidity on the capital structure: A case study of Croatian firms. *Business Systems Research, 3*(1), 30-36.

Scott J. (1977), "Bankruptcy, Secured Debt, and Optimal Capital Structure," *Journal of Finance Journal of Finance32 (1), 1-19.*

Sbeiti, Wafaa, (2010), "The Determinants of Capital Structure: Evidence from the GCC Countries", *International Research Journal of Finance and Economics, Issue 47, pp.1-27.*

Singh, D (2016) A Panel Data Analysis of Capital Structure Determinants: An Empirical Study of Non-Financial Firms in *Oman International Journal of Economics and Financial Issues, 2016, 6(4), 1650-1656.*

Strebulaev, I. A. & Kurshev, A. (2006) 'Firm Size and Capital Structure', EFA 2005

Strebulaev, I. A. & Yang, B. 2006, 'The Mystery of Zero-Leverage Firms', available at: http://papers.ssrn.com/sol3/papers.cfm?abstract_id=890719.

Suzan H & Nico Van der Wijist (2006): The Financing Structure of Non-listed companies: Discussion Paper No 468, Aug 2006, Statistics and Research department – Norway

Siti S Hussain M (2015) The Determinants of Capital Structure for Malaysian Food Producing Companies. *International Journal of Accounting and Business Management, Vol 1 no 1 p 1-26*

Songul K (2015); The Determinants of Capital Structure: Evidence from the Turkish Manufacturing Sector *International Journal of Economics and Financial Issues Vol. 5, No. 1, 2015, pp.158-171*

Titman, S. & Wessels, R. (1988), 'The Determinants of Capital Structure Choice' *Journal of Finance*, vol. 43, no. 1, pp. 1-19.

Thian C Lim, Xi'an Jiao tong (2012) Determinants of Capital Structure Empirical Evidence from Financial Services Listed Firms in China. *International Journal of Economics and Finance Vol. 4, No. 3*

Turki S and Alzomaia F (2014) Capital structure determinants of Publicly listed companies in Saudi Arabia. *The International Journal of Business and Finance Research, Vol 8, No 2, 53-67*

Uke M, Suhadak, Siti R and Solimun M (2014). The Influence of Company Size and Capital Structure towards Liquidity, Corporate Performance and Firm Value, for Large and Small Group Companies; *European Journal of Business and Management Vol.6, No.18, 2014*

Umar Butt (2016): Profits, Firm Size, Growth Opportunities and Capital Structure: An Empirical Test. *Journal of Finance and Economics Volume 4, 1 (2016), 58-69*

Velnampy T and Aloy J(2012) The Relationship between Capital Structure & Profitability. *Global Journal of Management and Business Research Volume 12 No 13(1)*

Wahab, S.N.A., Ramli, N.A. (2014), The Determinants of Capital Structure: An Empirical Investigation of Malaysian Listed Government Linked Companies, *International Journal of Economics and Financial Issues, 4(4), 930*

Zubairi, H.J. and Farooq, S. (2014) 'Factors influencing the capital structure in Pakistan', *Pakistan Business Review, Journal of Economic Literature, Vol. 16, No. 2, pp.211–231.*

APPENDICES

Appendix 1: Curriculum Vitae of the Researcher:

LUCKY YONA

Principal Consultant /Director of Research **Phone:** *+255 754 499307*
Eastern and Southern African Management of Institute **Email:** *yona_lucky@yahoo.com*
P.O.BOX 3030, Arusha, Tanzania

PERSONAL INFORMATION
Date of Birth: 23/07/1965
Nationality: Tanzanian
Gender: Male

SUMMARY OF EXPERIENCE

Lucky Yona is a Principal consultant and Director of Research and Publication. He holds a Doctorate degree in Business Administration (DBA), Master's Degree in Business Administration (MBA), Masters of Philosophy (MPHIL), Bachelor of commerce (BCOM) and Bachelor of Theology (B.Th.). He is also a Certified Public Accountant (CPA). He is an experienced consultant and International Trainer. Lucky has published five books in the area of finance and accounting, Corporate Finance, Taxation, International Finance and published numerous papers in international peer reviewed journals. Prior to joining ESAMI he has worked with various reputable institutions and companies in different senior capacities. He was previously the Financial Administrator (AMREF), Business Manager (International School of Moshi), College Bursar (Kilimanjaro Christian Medical College) and Chief Accountant (Iscor Mining). He has also taught at the Nyegezi Social Training Institute (Now St Augustine University in Tanzania). Lucky teaches the MBA courses at ESAMI Business School and specializes teaching in Financial Accounting, Corporate Finance, International Finance and Taxation. He was also the Africa Coordinator for the Rotterdam School of Management (RSM)/ESAMI Research Project on Inclusive business in Africa, a Project funded by Dutch Government involving eight countries (Kenya, Uganda, Tanzania, Mozambique, Rwanda and Ethiopia).

EDUCATION

Maastricht School of Management, Nerthelands
Doctor of Business Administration (DBA) 2016
Title: *The impact of Bank ownership on banking Competitiveness "Case of Tanzanian Banks.*
Masters of Philosophy (MPhil) 2014
Masters of Business Administration (MBA) 2005
University of Dar es Salaam
Bachelors of Commerce (Accounting), Honors 1991
National Board of Accountancy and Auditors 2005
Certified Public Accountant (CPA)

PUBLICATIONS
1. Yona L and Njoku J (2018) **The influence of Profitability on Company Leverage, Evidence from Tanzanian Listed and Unlisted Companies.** European Journal of Accounting, Auditing and Finance Research (EJAAFR); **Accepted 20. Dec 2017**
2. Yona L and Njoku J (2018) **The relationship between Asset Tangibility and leverage of Tanzanian companies.** Archives of Business Research Journal (ABR); **Accepted 15 Jan 2018**
3. Yona L and Njoku J (2018) **The influence of company liquidity on leverage: Case of Tanzanian Listed and Unlisted Companies**

European Journal of Accounting, Auditing and Finance Research (EJAAFR); **Accepted 20. Dec 2017**
4. Yona L and Njoku J (2018) **The influence of company size on leverage: Case of Tanzanian Listed and Unlisted Companies** European Journal of Accounting, Auditing and Finance Research (EJAAFR); **Accepted 25th Jan 2018**

Annex 2: Selected Listed Companies in Tanzania

Company	Year Listed	Nature of Business
TOL Gases Ltd. (TOL)	1998	Production and distribution of industrial gases, welding equipment's, medical gases, etc.
Tanzania Breweries Company	1990	Beverage Company
Tatepa Company Ltd. (TATEPA)	1999	Growing, processing, blending, marketing and distribution of tea and instant.
Tanzania Cigarette Company. (TCC)	2000	Manufacturing, marketing distribution and sale of cigarettes.
Tanga Cement Public Ltd Co.(SIMBA)	2002	Production, sale and marketing of cement.
Swissport Tanzania Ltd.	,2006	Airports handling of passengers and cargo.
Tanzania Portland Cement Co. Ltd. (TWIGA)	2006	Production, sale and marketing of cement.
Precision Air Services Plc	2011	Air transport services
Swala Gas and Oil	2014	Mineral Exploration
Kenya Airways Ltd. (KA)	2004	Passengers and cargo transportation to different destinations in the world
East African Breweries Ltd (EABL)	2005	Holding company of various companies involved in production, marketing and distribution of beer in Kenya, Uganda, Tanzania and Mauritius

National Media Group (NMG)	2011	News media group
Acacia Mining PLC	2011	Mining and production of gold

Source: Researcher 2015

Annex 3: **Selected Unlisted Companies in Tanzania**

1		BENSON COMPANY
2		THE SAFARI COMPANY
3		NEW SAFARI (1967) LTD
12		TANAPA COMPANY LTD
13		ACACIA MINING
14		ELEWANA AFRICA (T) LTD
15		TOURISM PROMOTION SERVICES (ZANZIBAR) LTD
16		COCACOLA KWANZA LTD
17		CMC AUTOMOBILE TANZANIA LTD
18		MULTISTRUCT (TANZANIA) LTD
19		TANZANIA PRINTERS LTD
20		PARKS ADVENTURE LTD
21		BONITE BOTTLERS LTD
22		BANYANGA AUTO GLASS LTD
23		MWANZA GROUP LTD
24		KIJUM0 CONSTRUCTION COMPANY LIMITED
25		DF MISTRY & CO. (1974)
26		KANJI LALJI CO LTD
27		OPHIR ENERGY PLC
28		MAERSK LOGISTICS TANZANIA LIMITED
29		TANZANIA BROADCASTING CORPORATION (TBC)
30		NABAKI AFRICA LTD
31		ACNIEL SEN TANZANIA LTD
32		XYZ TOBACCO COMPANY
33		DATAVISION INTERNATIONAL (DVI)
34		GIRAFFE OCEAN VIEW HOTEL
35		NSK TANZANIA LTD
36		TANELEC LIMITED (TANZANIA)
37		KAKAMURA COMPANY LTD
38		KIBO MINING PLC

39	TANZANIA TEA PACKERS LTD (TATEPA)
40	PANAFRICAN ENERGY TANZANIA LTD
41	ORCA ENERGY EXPLORATIONS
42	TANZANIA PETROLEUM DEVELOPMENT CORPORATION
43	NATIONAL HOUSING CORPORATION
44	MASANJA COMPANY
45	SERENGETI FRESH LIMITED
46	TANZANIA TOBACCO LTD

Source: Researcher 2017

www.ingramcontent.com/pod-product-compliance
Lightning Source LLC
Chambersburg PA
CBHW030741180526
45163CB00003B/872